REFRAMING MINISTRY LEADERSHIP

New Insights from a Systems Theory Perspective

ISRAEL GALINDO

Reframing Ministry Leadership
New Insights from a Systems Theory Perspective
Copyright © 2023, Israel Galindo
All rights reserved.

ISBN: 9798850907839

Published by Didache Press

CONTENTS

Introduction

FRAMEWORKS are mental models which represents your thought process about how things work in the real world. They contain concepts that interpret the world, rules about the relationships between its various parts, and your intuitive perception about how you act and engage in the world. A mental model helps explain "how things work." It is a worldview that you carry around in your mind to help you interpret your experience in the world and in your relationships.

Neuroscientist György Buzsáki wrote, "Once the mind has accepted a plausible explanation for something, it becomes a framework for all the information that is perceived after it. We're drawn, subconsciously, to fit and contort all the subsequent knowledge we receive into our framework, whether it fits or not. Psychologists call this "cognitive rigidity". The facts that built an original premise are gone, but the conclusion remains—the general feeling of our opinion floats over the collapsed foundation that established it. Information overload, "busyness," speed, and emotion all exacerbate this phenomenon. They make it even harder to update our beliefs or remain open-minded."[1]

Mental models are imperfect as they may contain biases, uncritical assumptions, and prejudices. This is why it's important that our mental models be informed by sound theory and critical thinking.

There is no single universal unifying mental model that provides a perfect explanation of the entire universe, or our experience of it. Mental models from various disciplines can provide frameworks to integrate and manage complex systems in our thinking.

We use mental models as frameworks every day, even when we are not aware of it. In fact, we've been building cognitive mental models since we were infants. We routinely add to our mental models, build on them, and revise them as we encounter new information and acquire more experiences. The concepts that make up our mental models can help us make wiser choices and take better actions. Sophisticated mental models, and their ensuing frameworks, are critical for anyone interested in thinking clearly, rationally, and effectively when leading an organization.

We all have a favorite mental model, the one we default to as an explanation for how or why something happened; for why people behave the way they do, for why we choose to do something, or not. As long as that mental model satisfies our need to come up with an explanation for a phenomenon, we will maintain it—

unquestioned and unexamined. Our brains are a bit lazy that way.

The problem is, when a particular mental model dominates our thinking, we'll try to explain every problem we face through that framework. This is a particular liability to those who are smart or expert in a given area. It explains, for example, why academics can be so brilliant in their fields, but so dumb about many other things. As the saying goes, "If all you have is a hammer, everything looks like a nail."

In this book faculty members of the Leadership in Ministry clergy leadership development program provide an opportunity to expand your mental model by "reframing" your thinking about leadership, ministry, and organizations. They use theoretical frameworks from organizational development research and from Bowen Systems Theory (BFST) in sharing their frameworks, and, how they have changed over time, especially as influenced by Bowen Systems Theory. Concepts from each of these frameworks will help you expand—perhaps even revise— your mental model about what it means to be a leader in your ministry organization.

NOTES

[1]György Buzsáki, "How the Brain 'Constructs' the Outside World," *Scientific American* (June 1, 2022).

I

REFRAMING MINISTRY
LEADERSHIP

1

Reframing Pastoral Leadership

Michael Lee Cook[1]

"Not all adults [leaders] are adult. Many who look grown-up on the outside may be childish on the inside. Others who look childish on the outside may be surprisingly mature on the inside." —H. A.Overstreet, The Mature Mind[2]

Darius Washington was called to pastoral leadership at Willow Creek Baptist Church in Sumpter, Tennessee two years ago. This is his twelfth year in the ministry and his second appointment as senior pastor. The first appointment lasted three years. He was asked to resign because of unresolved emotional issues that caused conflict with the congregation and its leadership. For legal reasons, this information was not shared with Willow Creek Baptist Church's search committee during the hiring process. In a recent meeting, Darius angrily exploded at the deacon board chair over concerns about his preaching and inability to connect with parishioners. This incident has left the church wondering if Darius was the right choice.

The importance of psychological and emotional maturity in leaders cannot be understated. It is far more important than technical knowledge or practical experience.[3] Yet, most leaders are commonly chosen based upon their work experience, knowledge, or training rather than their maturity. In my opinion, it should be otherwise.

This brief essay addresses the use of Bowen Family Systems Theory (BFST) to provide a framework for understanding leadership as an opportunity to become more self-differentiated (mature) and to develop emotionally and psychologically. Mature leaders can provide more effective leadership. This is especially true when church or community anxiety is intense.

In most cases, leadership is a deciding factor in the success or stagnation of any organization, including religious institutions. Every organization is an emotional system. That is, any part of an organization impacts every other part of the organization from an emotional standpoint. Leadership is a critical aspect of this dynamic. An organization will go no further than the level of differentiation of self (emotional maturity) of its leadership.

Every emotional system is different from others to some extent. So, success in one institution does not guarantee success in another organization. However, what is more consistent in importance from one institution to the next is the level of differentiation (maturity) in the leader. I think this is a reason leaders are better selected based upon their emotional maturity rather than their experience alone. Bowen Theory provides a way of understanding this dynamic and points a way for leaders to grow up and mature. The practice of leadership is a great context for this personal development.

Leadership Starts at Home

The families we grow up in have an enormous impact on our psychological and emotional development. That experience largely shapes the people we become. The impact of the nuclear family emotional system (family of origin) remains with us directly and indirectly throughout the course of our lives. Leaders carry the impact of their families of origin with them wherever they go.[4] So, to get clues about a leader's level of emotional development and functioning, it is important to gain an understanding and appreciation of their families of origin and their role in it.

Bowen understood the critical impact of the family emotional system to the development and functioning of individuals. He developed a tool, the family diagram (or genogram), to depict family relationships and track the emotional process(es) within the family system over multiple generations. This framework provided insights into relational patterns (e.g., fusion, cutoff, triangles, etc.) and their impact on the development of the individual and family. Bowen came to reason that people function in present relationships and emotional systems in similar ways in which they functioned in their families of origin.

This is a key insight into understanding the level of emotional maturity in leaders. It opens the door for leaders to evaluate their emotional, psychological, and relational development within the context of their families of origin and its impact on their present functioning in their role as leaders.

Anxiety a Key Variable

Bowen identified anxiety as a key variable in understanding how emotional systems shape individual and collective functioning. Anxiety is simply an instinctual and evolutionary dynamic that is present in all relationship systems, including organizations. Anxiety varies in degree, but not substance. This means that members of any relationship or emotional system are reactive to each other and on a continuum.

Reactivity is generally low when anxiety is minimal, but often increases when anxiety intensifies in the system and/or relationship. Any process or change that bumps up against its homeostasis (its normal level of emotional comfort) will raise the level of anxiety in the system and among its members. Leaders must be aware of the kinds of dynamics that impact the level of anxiety in their pastoral contexts and their own levels of reactivity to the changing intensity of anxiety.[5]

Generally, the greater the anxiety in a system, the greater reactivity among its members—particularly in individuals with lower levels of emotional maturity. For example, people usually manage their anxiety and reactivity to the extent of their differentiation of self (maturity). Leaders that are highly reactive to anxiety, both in themselves and the systems they lead, generally have lower levels of emotional maturity.

This factor can lead to less thoughtful pastoral functioning and ineffective leadership. Anxiety often exposes the level of maturity within leaders but can also present opportunities for emotional and psychological growing up.

Differentiation of Self (Maturity)

Differentiation of Self (maturity) is considered the cornerstone concept in Bowen Family Systems Theory (BFST). It is critical to understanding relationships and emotional systems and their impact on individual functioning.[6] In simple terms, it is about an individual's ability to function independently while remaining emotionally connected to others—particularly when anxiety is intense.

The concept is not only about learning how to differentiate (remain a distinct self) from others within emotional systems (e.g., family of origin), but also entails the ability to differentiate between one's thoughts and feelings. Both moves are considered marks of psychological maturity and often lead to better individual functioning and decision-making. The ability to differentiate self (mature functioning) is critical in the context of leadership.

It can often prove devastating to individuals and organizations when leaders have low levels of differentiation (maturity) while occupying positions with high degrees of responsibility and power.[7] Given that leadership often takes place in contexts with elevated levels of anxiety, it is an ideal setting to measure the extent of one's differentiation of self and provide opportunities to enhance it or grow oneself up emotionally.

Pastoral leaders do well to take advantage of this chance to mature themselves and impact their organizations positively. Differentiation of self is a lifelong process but can have an immediate impact on a leader's emotional functioning.[8]

Guided by Principles

In the intense environment of leadership, leaders need guideposts to help them negotiate the varying demands of people, resources, and ideas without losing themselves and their values. In Bowen theory, these guideposts are understood as guiding principles. Leaders must establish their own guiding principles based upon their deepest values and commitments.

Practically, this means mature leaders are guided more by well-thought-out principles rather than emotional reactivity. Fundamentally, guiding principles serve as filters for our thoughts, beliefs, and actions. They remain constant and rarely change regardless of the circumstances, context, or even the level of anxiety within emotional systems.

Principles help leaders gain the distance necessary for objectivity in decision-making when anxiety is high, and reactivity is prominent. For example, a guiding principle could be that you make important decisions only after careful consideration of the facts, not by the demands of the crowd.

Furthermore, guiding principles can be drawn upon in moments of stress and anxiety. They also allow leaders to develop boundaries for themselves as well as for the people and organizations they lead. Leaders must have principles to guide their actions, reactions, and thinking. This is particularly important in contexts and situations that are anxiety intensive.

The act and process of taking accountability and thinking deeply and seriously about our guiding principles of life and leadership is a deep sign of maturity. The process can help us grow up and strengthen our level of differentiation of self. In turn, this can prepare us to be more effective and emotionally connected leaders.

Without a doubt, principles also help keep leaders from overfunctioning (taking responsibility for things that do not belong to them) and/or underfunctioning (asking others to take responsibility for things that belong to them) in the context of their lives and work.

Commitment to Mature

Bowen theory teaches that maturing is an ever-unfolding process. There is no moment in time when maturing is complete. Maturity must be worked for. This is certainly true in the context of leadership. To this end, leaders must make a commitment to mature (grow up) beyond their levels of current maturity as a way of shoring up their capacity to lead effectively.

The level of maturity that gets a leader a job will not be enough to help the leader maintain and be successful on the job. This is essentially the case because every emotional system (e.g., congregation) will often require a different level of maturity from its leadership. Namely, because of its level of anxiety, stress, and insistence on maintaining homeostasis.

And maturity can happen best in places that push us beyond our emotional comfort zones. For example, person-to-person relationships can be an important way of growing up and maturing. Bowen thought that it was helpful to work on individual relationships that are usually the most difficult.[9] The thought being that this gives us a great chance to gauge where we stand in our emotional development and maturity and presents an opportunity to grow our levels of differentiation of self.

Ultimately, a commitment to mature is about developing the capacity to become a more objective-observer of the emotional systems we are a part of; strengthening our capacity to make decisions guided by facts more than feelings; and creating more of a Self in relationships while remaining emotionally connected to others.

Conclusion

Leadership is fundamentally an opportunity to grow up and mature as individuals. In fact, leading often challenges old assumptions and deeply held beliefs about the Self and the world around us. These emotional and social dynamics can often hinder and/or expand our emotional and psychological maturity.

This can make a huge difference for individuals and organizations alike. Thus, leaders have a first obligation to work on themselves emotionally. This can lead to more maturity, credibility, and effectiveness in leading others. Given this perspective, leaders would be better selected based on their levels of differentiation of self versus their resumes and experiences alone.

The process of psychological change and maturing will continue for a lifetime. Old habits and unfinished emotional work are very challenging to overcome. But with time, patience, practice, and persistence, heightened maturity is possible. In the end, maturing is an intentional process. It is not a given. Leadership provides an opportunity to do the work in whatever context(s) it takes place. The quest is not ultimately about leading people alone, but about learning how to maturely lead and manage Self and Self alone.

For Reflection:

1. *How do you think growing up in your family of origin impacts the way you emotionally function as a leader?*
2. *What is your typical response to anxious situations?*
3. *To what extent are you able to function without seeking the approval or affirmation of others?*
4. *What are your guiding principles regarding life and leadership?*

5. *How committed are you to growing your own emotional and psychological maturity?*
6. *What will you do with your opportunity to mature?*

NOTES

[1]Michael Lee Cook, ThD, LMFT is a licensed marriage and family therapist and Bowen Coach in private practice at Micah Counseling Services in Tyrone, Georgia. Michael provides counseling and consulting to individuals, couples, families, and organizations. He also serves as a faculty coach in the Leadership in Ministry program.

[2] Overstreet, H.A., *The Mature Mind* (New York: W.W. Norton & Company, Inc., 1949), 19.

[3]Friedman, Edwin., *A Failure of Nerve: Leadership in the Age of the Quick Fix* (Church Publishing, Inc., 2007), 17.

[4] Brown, Jenny Brown., *Growing Yourself Up: How to bring your best self to all of life's relationships* (Australia: Exisle Publishing Pty, Ltd., 2017), 48-49.

[5] Kerr, Michael E., *Bowen Theory's Secrets: Revealing the Hidden Life of Families* (New York: W.W. Norton & Company, 2019), 171-172.

[6] Gilbert, Roberta M., *Extraordinary Relationships: A New Way of Thinking About Human Interactions* (New York: John Wiley & Sons, Inc., 1992), 18.

[7] Friedman, Edwin H., *A Failure of Nerve: Leadership in the Age of the Quick Fix* (Church Publishing, Inc., 2007), 155.

[8] Papero, Daniel V., *Bowen Family Systems Theory* (Massachusetts: Allyn and Bacon, 1990), 48.

[9] Bowen, Murray., *Family Therapy in Clinical Practice* (New York: Jason Aronson, Inc., 1978), 540-541.

2

Reframing Success in Ministry

Meg Hess

When I hear the word success, the old song by Bill Deal and the Rhondels starts playing in my head, "Nothing Succeeds Like Success." The song tells the story of a young man who casts his love aside in pursuit of fame and riches, hoping that when he gets to the top of the ladder of success, she might still be there waiting for him. It's the soundtrack of the American dream where the yardstick of success measures accomplishments in more money, power, prestige, influence, and the accumulation of material goods. Success is defined in measurements of bigger, better, and more than. Success is understood in the context of competition and comparison.

How do we measure success in ministry? I first became a pastor in 1980 when there were very few ordained women pastoring Baptist churches. A story about my first call to a pastorate in the local newspaper inferred that the church called me, a woman, because they couldn't afford a man. If women ministers found a pastoral call at all, it was most often to a small, struggling church that the more "successful" pastors were not interested in serving. Success in that ministerial context was seen as being called to a large, thriving church with a big budget, multiple staff members and a minister who had a doctorate and was renowned in the denomination as a stellar preacher.

I bought into that definition of ministry success in my early years. I assumed that if I worked hard enough that I, too, would climb the ministry ladder of success and move from a small church to a mid-sized church to a bigger church with a bigger staff and then, of course, to a "flagship" church. "Nothing succeeds like success, and I guess, I want to be just like all of the rest…" goes the song. Somewhere along the way I let go of that definition of success. That was due in part to the reality of the stained-glass ceiling for women in ministry. Those bigger, better churches were slow to call women as their pastors, saying things like: "Well, we'd consider a woman for this position but there aren't any with enough experience yet." When the women ministers finally got those years of experience under their belt, the flagship churches would call young, married men with children and little pastoral experience to be their pastor. Because, well, Church Growth.

Shifting my framework of success in ministry involved much more than my coming to terms with my resentment about the barriers that women in ministry faced. As I began to reframe my measurements for success my desires for those external measures of success diminished. Through many years of working with Bowen Family Systems Theory, my definition of success has been reshaped and my framework about both success and failure has come into clearer focus. External markers of success—size of congregation, budget, or reputation—have been replaced by values and principles that are much harder to measure: maturity in self and in the system, deepening of capacities of emotional intelligence, ability to differentiate a self in the leadership position, and an increased ability to self-regulate so that I may function more effectively in the pastoral role.

Working on Yourself

While pastoring a church, I was in psychotherapy, spiritual direction, a peer supervision group for therapists, and a clergy women's support group. I remember thinking "What is wrong with me that I need so much support in order to be in ministry?" When I added the Leadership in Ministry Workshops to this list, I began to shift my assessment of my self-care and on-going educational practices. Instead of thinking about these activities as an expression of weakness, I reframed them as expressions of

working on my Self. A critical part of occupying the
pastoral role is the commitment to one's own growth,
maturity, and personal and professional development. My
understanding of Self is informed by Bowen's concepts of
Pseudo-self and Solid-self.

Pseudo-self and Solid-self

My Field Education experience in seminary placed
a lot of emphasis on accepting one's "pastoral identity."
Stepping into the pastoral role, claiming the authority of
the pastoral office, and learning to identify the
expectations of self and others were a significant part of
the ministerial formation process. I spent my early years in
ministry putting on that ministerial mantle. When I
stepped out of full-time congregational ministry for a
season after we adopted our daughter, I noticed the many
ways in which I had overidentified with the pastoral role.
If I wasn't The Reverend Dr. Hess after twenty years of
ministry, then who was I?

Bowen systems theory provides a lens to examine
our attachment to the ministerial role in its concept of
Pseudo-Self. According to Michael Kerr, "Pseudo-self is
made up of principles, beliefs, philosophies, and
knowledge that people acquire because the important
groups they are a part of consider the beliefs and other
ideas to be correct. Pressure from a group to incorporate its
ideas come in many forms and with varying degrees of

intensity."[1] Kerr wrote, "Pseudo-self is negotiable in a relationship system, meaning a person will disavow or discard a belief or principle in face of emotional pressure to do so." Clergy are always navigating being a faithful representative of a religious tradition and being true to their interpretation of that tradition. Defining a self in a religious context at times may involve departing from the group interpretation of theology as one clarifies and expresses one's thinking and beliefs.

Kerr wrote, "A hallmark of pseudo-self is people pretending to be something they are not."[2] Clergy who over-identify with their role are at mercy of other's projections and expectations. Someone once joked that clergy wear the little white square on their clerical collar because it serves as a convenient screen for people's projections. Sometimes I think that 90% of our job as a pastoral leader is to identify those projections and to manage our reactivity to them. Clergy pretending to be something or someone they are not can vary from being pious to presenting as competent (or incompetent) to hiding what we really believe to losing touch with a sense of their core identity. This pretense makes us vulnerable to being seduced by people's projections into believing that we are far more, or less, than we truly are as human beings.

Kerr noted that, "Another feature of pseudo-self is holding discrepant beliefs." When we hold contradictory beliefs, or when the gap between our "espoused" theology and our "operative" theology is wide, then we are functioning out of pseudo-self. Kerr proposes that "…the need for attention, acceptance, and meeting perceived expectations is so powerful in human beings that the feeling system bypasses or overwhelms the important process of cognitive dissonance in rational thinking."[3] The antidote to pseudo-sel, according to Kerr, is to grow one's Solid Self.

The Solid Self is expressed when one takes a clear "I-position" in a relational system. Differentiating a Solid Self occurs in the interplay between one's internal intellectual system and their feeling/emotional system. According to Bowen theory: "Solid self reflects a functional intellectual system. It enables a person to withstand pressure from the emotional/feeling system. Solid self is made up of firmly held convictions, principles, and beliefs that are formed slowly during development." Bowen noted that the Solid self is formed in the complex interaction of these two internal systems. "The 'self' is composed of constitutional, physical physiological, biological, genetic, and cellular reactivity factors, as they move in unison with psychological factors."[4] Cultivating the capacity to think clearly about one's guiding principles, values, and beliefs while working with one's emotional/feeling system is a significant aspect of understanding Solid self.

Success and Differentiation of Self as a Ministerial Leader

The process of distinguishing pseudo-self from Solid self informs my framework about Differentiation of Self in the leadership context. Based on the thinking of Edwin Friedman, Lawrence Matthews, pastor and founder of the Leadership In Ministry program, taught that differentiation of self as a leader involves three dimensions: self-definition, self-regulation, and staying connected to everyone in the System.

Self-Definition

Being able to define a self involves knowing what one thinks, believes, values, and cherishes. Self-definition requires that one articulate their guiding principles when taking a stand or providing guidance to a congregation. Self-definition means being able to say, "Here's how I see it," and "Here's what I'd like to see happen."

Self-definition also involves clarity about one's role and function in the system. Lawrence Matthews often asked, "What is your role here?" He went on to say, "If you don't know what your role is as Pastor, then there will be at least 50 or more people who will be happy to tell you what your role is." Occupying the "L" (Leadership) position requires being aware of the expectations others may have of your role. A clearly defined understanding of your leadership role requires developing the capacity to tolerate the displeasure of others when you don't meet their expectations about your pastoral role and function.

Self-Regulation

Differentiating a Self requires the ability to self-regulate. When one makes a differentiating or self-defining move in a system it is not unusual to encounter push-back from the system. That push-back can trigger anxiety in the one taking a stand as they resist the pull of the togetherness force and the system's desire to return to homeostasis.

Anxiety, the normal response to a threat, can be real or imagined. The brain can't always tell the difference. The responses most common to anxiety are fight, flight, freeze, flock, fawn, or fix. Bringing awareness to your typical responses to anxiety is one step in learning how to self-regulate while holding a clear leadership stance. The aim of down-regulation is to protect one's thinking from being hijacked by the emotional/feeling system. Every leader has their own unique way of supporting their capacity to self-regulate. Prayer, meditation, creating a healthy work-life fit, exercise, nurturing sustaining personal relationships, and expressing creativity and play are just a few of the paths to self-care, which makes regulating one's emotional reactivity more sustainable.

A leader can have internal anxious reactivity and yet still function in a thoughtful way guided by principles and values. In terms of Bowen's metaphorical Differentiation of Self Scale, your basic self can experience its reactivity at a lower level while self-regulation can help you to function a little higher up the scale. Working toward less-reactive functioning is a step along the way toward the goal of achieving Friedman's ideal of being a non-anxious presence in the leadership position.

Staying Connected

Differentiation of self in leadership also involves staying emotionally connected with the congregation while self-defining and self-regulating. If the norm in your family of origin is to use distance as a strategy to deal with difference and conflict, then staying connected will be more of a challenge to you. One doesn't differentiate a self in isolation, but within the context of an interconnected system. The process of leadership development is a continual dance of moving through these three aspects of Differentiation. And just when you think it is settled, the process of taking a stand, regulating self in the face of resistance, and staying connected starts all over again. Differentiation of self in leadership is a constant, dynamic, work-in-progress.

Reframing my understanding of Differentiation of Self in leadership has given me a new reference point for assessing my "success" as a ministerial leader. For me, moving from pseudo-self to Solid self through my attempts to differentiate a self while leading has become more important than the external measures of success.

Whether I serve as an Interim Minister or Settled Pastor, a Pastoral Psychotherapist, Life Coach, or Teacher, my focus is on upleveling my emotional maturity as I function in any of those ministerial roles. Taking responsibility for myself, consulting my principles, developing my thinking, tending to self so that my anxious reactivity isn't driving the bus, and making the effort to connect emotionally to others in the system are the markers of my success in ministry.

Bill Deal's song about success says: "nothing succeeds like success and I guess, I wanna be just like all of the rest..." But my work with BFST has helped me conclude that I don't wanna to be just like all of the rest. I want to be myself as a leader, at home in my own skin, authentically congruent both in and out of the pulpit, seeking to take full responsibility for my actions, thinking, and emotional states even as I support others in becoming their true, solid self.

What is success in the congregational setting?

As my understanding of success for myself as a ministerial leader has shifted, my framework about what a successful congregation looks like has changed as well. As the importance of external measures of success such as numbers, financial viability, and relevance become less important in my thinking, a different focus emerges. I am now more concerned with supporting congregations in developing capacities for mature functioning in their interactions with one another and in their mission to the world. I strive to emulate Parker Palmer's challenge to lead in a way that models "no fixing, no saving, no advising, and no setting each other straight."[5] In my last Interim Pastorate, I shifted the focus of my work from problem solving to promoting maturity in the congregational system. Here are some of the places I now focus my thinking and efforts:

- Helping congregations understand their origin stories and how their founding has influenced their multi-generational process of becoming who they are today
- Assessing a congregation's need for capacity building. For example, working with a conflict avoidant congregation to develop more capacity to tolerate discomfort with differences and to practice taking clear, defining position with one another.
- Inviting leaders to observe where anxiety is most likely to show up in the system
- Inviting leaders to notice who plays what role around anxiety (generator, amplifier, absorber, distributor, or thoughtful self-regulator of anxiety)
- Clarifying their values and guiding principles as they make decisions
- Working with the people who are functioning in a healthy way and who are ready to do the work of transformation

- Not over-focusing on the problem people
- Pointing out patterns that repeat throughout their history and inviting the congregation to get curious about underlying dynamics
- Exploring with the leaders how anxiety gets both bound and distributed in the system by the triangulation process
- Modeling how to distinguish the content of messages from emotional process in their functioning
- Challenging leaders to adapt creatively to changing circumstances rather than accommodate to the most anxious and least functional members
- Inviting the congregation to identify strengths and resources in their historical narrative.

In summary, it is through attending faithfully to understanding and working creatively with the emotional process in the congregation that I am most likely to move toward the success of supporting mature functioning by myself, the congregation, and its leaders. St. Ignatius referred to the church as "a school for the affections." Using that metaphor, a successful congregation is a place of learning to be fully human, where the intellectual and emotional/feeling systems are in deep conversation with one another.

Reframing Failure

Reframing success in ministry contains within it the invitation to reframe failure. Simply, failure may be defined as the lack of success. Failure is usually accompanied by feelings of shame and diminished self-worth. Our sense of meaning, purpose, and value can be jeopardized by failure and our goals derailed. Or we can think differently about "failure." As poet and playwright Samuel Beckett said, "Try again. Fail again. Fail better." Beckett challenges us to reframe failure into an opportunity to deepen our learning and growth. Instead of thinking of failure as a Period, it can become a Comma, or Semicolon. Failure invites us to become curious about what really happened, to take a bigger view of the situation.

When I flamed out in my first pastorate I felt like a complete failure in ministry. Thanks to the support of loving mentors who believed in me when I couldn't believe in myself, I chose to get curious instead of quitting. I started studying BFST to try and understand what happened. Broadening my framework to "think systems" helped me to shift from shame and blame of self and others to a more compassionate exploration of complex dynamics. Changing my framework helped me to take ownership of my own mistakes and missteps without buying into the false belief that everything that went wrong was my fault. Pema Chodron says, "failure can be the portal to creativity, to learning something new, to having a fresh perspective."[6] My failures in ministry were the portal into "growing myself up," developing new capacities, inching my way up the scale of Differentiation of Self.

Accepting my failures as significant contributions to my maturation process has enhanced, if only slightly, my capacity to move from shame through learning to growth. The grace that allows for self-compassion and the permission to fail, fail again, and fail better are generous companions on the journey to bring my full, authentic Self into ministry. The poet Antonio Machado puts it beautifully:

> Last night as I was sleeping,
> I dreamt—marvelous error!—
> that I had a beehive
> here inside my heart.
> And the golden bees
> were making white combs
> and sweet honey
> from my old failures.[7]

So may it be.

NOTES

[1]Michael Kerr, *Bowen Theory's Secrets: Revealing the Hidden Lives of Families* (W. W. Norton & Company, 2019), p. 50.

[2]Kerr, *Bowen Theory's Secrets*, p. 51.

[3]Kerr, *Bowen Theory's Secrets*, p. 52.

[4]Michael Kerr and Murray Bowen, Kerr, *Family Evaluation: An Approach Based on Bowen Theory* (W. W. Norton & Company, 1988), p. 342.

[5]Parker Palmer, *A Hidden Wholeness; The Journey Toward an Undivided Life* (San Francisco: Jossy-Bass, 2004).

[6]Pema Chodron, 2014. Commencement address at Naropa University.

[7]Antonia Machado. *Border of a Dream*. Trans. by Willis Barnstone. 2004. p. 87.

II

REFRAMING MINISTRY PRACTICES

3

Reframing the Helping Relationship: When is Helping Helpful and When is it Not?

Vanessa Ellison

The theme of the seminary I attended was "Servant Leadership." Each convocation had a pottery bowl and hand towel placed on the altar as a visual representation of servant leadership. Worship services throughout the year included songs and hymns about being a servant leader. At graduation graduates received a hand towel with one's name embroidered on it as a physical reminder of the call to be a servant leader.

I took this metaphor too literal as a new minister straight out of seminary, and in doing so I gave too much of myself away – as if I indeed was a literal servant. I am not talking about giving *of* one's self but of giving *up* one's self. Even when Jesus was crucified as the ultimate sacrifice, he was still fully himself. He had given *of* himself but not give *up* who he was. If anything, the clarity of who he was drove what he did.

I do not think my seminary professors would have said, "Go into the world and be a no self," but that is sometimes what happens in the name of helping. Throughout my career as a minister and licensed clinical social worker, I have seen other ministers and helping professionals act from that framework. This kind of help is driven by the helper's need to be—or appear—helpful, useful, needed, or feel validated, loved, seen, heard, adored, etc.

From a Bowen Theory framework, we say this kind of help is driven by unresolved emotional process. It is not driven by clarity of self and guiding principles. This results in unclear expectations and boundaries, the inability to take appropriate stands, too much advice giving, over explaining, coercing, coddling, over focusing on feelings and empathy, and persuading others to do what the helper thinks is best. This kind of help ends up being quite unhelpful.

Helping as natural and instinctual

Helping ranges from giving advice to providing hospitality to defining the function or status of one's place in a profession. The essence is that one entity, the helper, is doing and/or providing something to/for another, "the helpee," to improve a situation and/or state of being for another person, people group, community, or society.

Helping is a natural and instinctual reciprocal process between two entities – the helper and the helpee – in which neither can exist without the other. Bees, red foxes, mole rats, and prairie dogs are examples of social systems that have members with designated roles who help through feeding, grooming, protecting, and even entertaining other members in order for the whole system to survive.[1] Likewise with humans, society depends on helping for its survival, development, and nourishment: a mother nursing her baby who is unable to feed himself, an uncle providing financial assistance for a niece to attend college, a doctor performing cardiac surgery, a teacher teaching young children to read, a social worker lobbying for housing equality in his city, a psychotherapist providing a way for a client to process their past, and a minister who is present day in and day out with their congregants and community providing religious sacraments, pastoral care, and faith development. Social systems cannot survive without one helping and another being helped. The helping dynamic is innate in the structure for survival.

The dilemma is distinguishing when is helping helpful and how – and when is it not? When does helping not improve a situation or state of being for another person, group, community, or society and actually work against it? When and how do helpers and helping agencies get in the way of another person's, family's, group's, and community's growth? How does it further enable the dependency on the helper/helpee dynamic?

Helping that is not helpful

Murray Bowen conducted the National Institution of Mental Health (NIMH) Family Study Project from 1954-1959 with people who experienced schizophrenia and with their families. Early into the study, he observed that clinicians telling the families what to do was not helpful.[2] Instead of enabling them to function better, family members transferred their emotional process onto the helper, who at times, accepted the countertransference.

Bowen and Butler explain, "The mother and child used their relationships with staff to *escape* the problem implicit in their intense relationship."[3] As such, the problem was outside of the family unit, and the helper became a part of the emotional process. In cases such as this, the work becomes focused on what the helper could do for the helpee, further hindering the family's work.

I once worked in a local non-profit that aimed to empower families to utilize their strengths and internal resources while collaborating with external resources to address the challenges in their family. The emphasis was on what *the family* thought they needed to help their family. They considered recommendations and resources from helpers while identifying what they thought was best. Some families latched on to this and began to strive. Problems arose, however, with the number of helpers assisting the family – a therapist, a school representative, a probation officer, a social worker *and*, a group home representative for the child; a therapist for one parent, a therapist for another, a therapist for the couple, a therapist for the family etc. The families were overloaded with numerous meetings and conflicted requirements. They were told what to do by helpers and/or the court, thus losing their agency – and for some a sense of dignity. Many felt defeated after identifying resources and solutions to addressing their family's concerns only to be told no and what to do instead.

Helping can be unhelpful when:

- Parents make their child go to therapy without participating in it themselves; do things for their children that the children can do for themselves; or shelter their children from the realities of the world out of their own fears.
- Clinicians are available to their clients at any time for anything; side with one client over another; or try to be friends with their clients.
- Ministers tell congregants what to believe and condemn anyone who believes differently; use cliches to describe a person's grieving process; or blame one person for the problems of the congregation.

- Dioceses located in a heavily populated city telling parishes in rural areas what to do—denominations telling congregations what their focus needs to be for the year—without realizing that the needs may be different depending on demographics, mission, and vision.
- Teachers who focus on meeting quotas over teaching; schools that change their policies whenever parents complain; or school boards that begin to side with one parent or group.
- The organization that enters a community to implement a program without considering if it will work with that community; oversteps its boundaries; or puts unrelated requirements on helpees in order to receive services.
- Agencies overworking helpers by giving them more responsibilities with more clients and fewer resources; focusing on numbers more than quality care; or ignoring vicarious trauma.

Helpers do not set out thinking they will actually get in the way of a person's growth. Each brings their training, expertise, and experiences with the idea that they will help change other people's situations for the better. Elaine Boomer, a Leadership in Ministry (LIM) coach, describes over-functioning as having goals for another that they do not have for themselves. Most helpers want the best for the people they are helping; however, helping can run the risk of over-functioning when it *is not* what the person, family, or group needs or want, hinders them, or causes more harm.

Mary-Frances O'Connor writes in *The Grieving Brain*, "I think advice is exactly what makes grieving people hold at arm's length those who would like to help them. People are experts of their own grief, their own life, their own relationships."[4]

Many theories hold that a lack of empathy is what hinders helpees; however, this is not part of the framework of Bowen Theory. Empathy can encourage a helper to ponder what it may be like to be in a helpee's shoes, but, like over-functioning, it runs the risk of joining in the emotional process. Edwin Friedman cautioned that empathy "serves as a rationalization for the inability of those in helping positions to develop self-control and not enable or interfere, a disguise for unacknowledged anxiety that desires a quick fix, and an indulgence for those who are not in a position where they have to make tough decisions."[5] What has led to a person's and family's predicament, symptoms, or inappropriate behaviors is a complicated matter that occurred over a multigenerational process with variables of levels of differentiation of self, chronic anxiety, and prolonged stress. Helpers that assume the "answers are simple and straightforward" miss this.[6]

Helping that seeks to tell others what to do, makes demands more than invite and encourage, blames the leader, focuses on one person, does not consider what a family thinks will be helpful, etc. is not helpful. This kind of help assumes there are quick fixes, creates and enables a dependency on the helper, gets in the way of people taking responsibility for themselves, and neglects to see the complexity of the problem – and ability to solve it – in the family unit. It is also driven by the helper's unresolved emotional process more than a genuine desire to help others.

Reframing Helping – The Helper

How then is one to understand helping – especially as it is inherent to the survival of humanity? Bowen Theory maintains that the work begins with the helper's own work toward differentiation of self. As Bowen began to work on his own functioning with his family in and following the NIMH Family Study Project, clinicians began to do the same—and asked him for advice on what to do. That began the coaching dynamic that continues to be a fundamental part of Bowen Theory today. Bowen began to see a correlation to the clinician's ability to remain out of, rather than join in, the unresolved emotional process of the family unity *and* the family's ability to improve its functioning. Families were freed up to focus on their own functioning *when helpers* could take responsibility for self, remain neutral and supportive, not take on the role of the parents, and be curious and engaging.

Bowen Theory is not unique in focusing on the need for helpers to work on one's self. Training programs for pastoral care, chaplains, clinicians, and psychotherapists challenge trainees to explore what brought them into the profession, what they get out of helping, and unresolved emotional processes that may affect their work—and to continue this work through continuing education units throughout one's career. The emphasis of continuing education, however, often is more on how the helpee is affected than it is on the helper's work on self. I was often reminded while working towards my licensure that the helping professional's license is there to protect helpees, telling them that the helper "meets the state's *minimal* qualifications" to perform the given tasks. It does not indicate the quality of those services and/or the helper's work on self. With Bowen theory, the helper works towards differentiation of self *throughout* one's life; it is not a one-time thing that a person does to complete a course, get a degree, and/or have an experience. It is lifelong work, and the helper's ability to help others derives out of this.

"Who in your family called you into ministry?" is a common question asked at LIM workshops. In other words, how were you formed so that you naturally navigated to a helping profession, and who in your family reinforced this and how? What are the strengths of this natural instinct? What are the challenges? And how can these get in the way of another's work towards differentiation of self?

Michael Kerr defines emotional programming as the "transmission of information across the generations in a family by relationships and learning" that "results from verbal, nonverbal, and behavioral interactions that occur within and between the generations."[7] Individuals become emotionally programmed through relationships with a wide array of family members, but most particularly with their role and function in the parental triangle and sibling position. This influences how one comes to need attention, approval, and/or acceptance; how they conform to expectations; and how they react to distress in the system. Emotional programming is not conscious; rather, it derives from instinctual patterned ways of functioning in relationships. This is neither good nor bad; rather a description of what is. What did I seek from my father? What did I seek from my mother? What did I seek from my siblings?

A three old does not say, "I get mommy's attention by being her special little boy," "Daddy expects too much from me, and I will never live up to his expectations," or "I wish my little brother would stop taking all of mommy's attention and being a brat." Instead, these become evident by looking at the reciprocal patterns of the system. The three-year-old senses the distress in the home. He does not know what it is called, but he follows directions, says "please" and "thank you," is happy, delights in his mother patting him on the head and calling him her "good little boy," and likes when his father laughs when he is silly with his little brother. In return, the parents are calmer with the stress of rearing two young boys while both working full time jobs. They consider themselves lucky to have such a "good little boy" who is a help to the family. In return, they give him more and more responsibilities as he grows, and he lives up to them. The brothers grow up each distinguishing themselves in different ways, but the eldest gets noticed in his extended family, school, and community as being a fine remarkable young man who helps his family and community. He may even become a helping professional!

This individual has been emotionally programmed to be thoughtful, considerate, polite, a resource to others, and aware of how his actions affect others. He has also been emotionally programmed to get attention by being good, gets approval by meeting expectations, acceptance by not bringing more stress to the system and instead contributing to the system's wellbeing. The person is not a victim; nor are his parents or brother the villains. Each played a part in this dynamic, and more than likely, it was a pattern repeated in previous generations. The extent to which this affects the person depends on the person's and family's level of differentiation of self and the chronic anxiety passed down through the multigenerational process.

The religious tradition and culture in which I was reared placed an emphasis on being "called." What is God calling you to do? While people said that everyone is called by God to do something, there was more celebration and focus on those who were called into ministry; it was perceived as a "special status." Ministers are not immune to this—other helping professionals experience it too. Society further solidifies this special status with freebies, discounts, and hallmark holidays. Some helpers find that their special status was reinforced in their families as being the golden child, or meant to do great things. Others were on the outside fringes of their families and helping gave them a place or role they did not have at home. For some, being a helper is seen as rebellion against the family, community, and/or society. Their parents had higher, grander aspirations or different expectations than congregational, non-profit, or social services work. Each of these reasons—golden child, safe haven, and rebellion— reinforce a person's need for acknowledgment, acceptance, and approval. This is not to undermine a person's calling into a vocation; but it is important to recognize the emotional programming that is a part of the process that brings a helper into the helping profession—and affects how they continue to function in the role of helper.

On the one end of the spectrum is a helper not grounded in self who leads out of their need for approval, attention, and acceptance, reactivity to expectations, and an intolerance for distress. They are unable to separate who they are from their identity as a helper. Bowen Theory calls this a "pseudo self" in which the person borrows and trades self from other people, ideas, or beliefs. Here are just a few examples:

- The minister who struggles setting boundaries with an inappropriate congregant out of fear that someone may get mad and not approve.
- The therapist who overshares out of their need to be liked and accepted.
- The teacher who over works to get the principal's attention.
- The chaplain who misses key elements of a case due to the organization's high expectations for the number of clients.

Even the most mature person borrows self, but a more grounded person is aware of what and from whom and where self is being borrowing. A helper grounded in who they are, in their "solid self," can see this and readjust accordingly. They can be clear about their emotional programming and use it as a framework to think systems, be aware of the emotional field, see multigenerational reciprocal processes, be curious, and engage another's best thinking. They can remain neutral, lead out of guiding principles, and distinguish their role in the overall dynamics to see what is and is not helpful.[8]

Reframing Helping – The Helper's work with the Helpee

So, what is helpful? There is not a Bowen Theory definition for helping, but here are some of my thoughts based upon my studies and practice of the theory over the years.

Helping empowers others towards differentiation of self. A professional helper in Bowen Theory is called a coach. This is not the same as a life coach which helps individuals work towards life goals in career, health, living skills, etc. A Bowen Theory coach is someone who first and foremost works toward differentiation of self in all spheres of their life. They can coach another person to do the same, not because they tell others what to do or how to do it; rather, they understand what a helpee is up against in their efforts to working toward differentiation of self. They help "guide… away from unprofitable trial and error wandering" by remaining neutral and utilizing the theory to help helpees engage their best thinking.[9] They are not focused on outcome—i.e. whether the couple stays together, if the minister is able to increase the membership of the congregation, if the nonprofit raises millions of dollars, etc.—but working towards differentiation of self for one's self and to assist others in their efforts to do the same. They do this from a family systems approach, not an individual one.

Helping understands problems are symptoms of a reciprocal emotional process in a system and does not seek to blame individuals. Helpers remain neutral and do not take sides. The presenting problem is often *not* the problem or one person; rather it is a system's—i.e., the family, congregation, or organization's—capacity to adapt and function around challenges and prolonged stress. Each person has a role and function within the system that affects the systems' functioning.

Remaining neutral allows helpers to ask challenging questions that promote differentiation of self of the family and its members. Edwin Friedman writes that leaders have a failure of nerve when they look for a quick fix, blame others, side with others, and are reactive.[10] Being neutral can be challenging when one has experienced violence from another in the same system. The person who experienced the violence *is not* to blame for the situation. At the same time, exploring the reciprocal dynamics over several generations can help to understand what led to and perpetuates the violence, and how the family may change its functioning. Similarly, one person in a relationship is not primarily or singularly responsible when a partner cheats on them. Understanding that relationships are reciprocal yields the question, "What is occurring in the relationship that creates a scenario for one person to step out on another?" Blaming one person or focusing only on the problem allows others not to focus on their own functioning and perpetuates the system's problems.

Helping assists helpees in their efforts to get clear for themselves by identifying challenges, opportunities, and resources in the process—not by telling another person what to do, think, or believe. This is not to say that a Bowen Theory coach never tells someone what to do. If or when they do, the emphasis is on helping the person to access their best thinking and/or improve their self-regulation, so that they can better understand, think, and engage relationships and situations. Similarly, this does not mean that the helper will not express an opinion. The helper can define self— "This is what I think," "I hear you, but I disagree," or "This is where I stand,"—without needing the other person to think the same. The principle is that a person is the expert of their own life. While I may understand and see things differently as a clinician who specializes in Bowen Theory, only my clients know what it is like for them in their lives, and therefore, can determine what is best for them. Robert Noone states, "A coach, grounded in Bowen theory, can serve as a resource in the effort, but the responsibility lies with the individual interested in making the effort and the primary relationship in this process is with the family and not the coach."[11]

Helping engages the helpee's best thinking more than focusing on feelings. Emotional identification can help a person see and understand bigger pictures when it is considered as *one* piece of information amongst other factors, like the level of differentiation of self, chronic anxiety, prolonged stress, resources, principles, etc. But over focusing on feelings is not helpful. It is somewhat paradoxical, but the less helpers focus on feelings and empathy, the more they can remain neutral, can avoid taking sides, or avoid entering the helpee's emotional process. Furthermore, they can be *more* present and *better* assist the helpee to engage their endeavors towards differentiation of self by taking a stance of curiosity, focusing on facts, and not being afraid to ask questions that may not make them feel good in the moment but will engage their thinking towards better functioning over a lifetime.

Helping utilizes the system as a resource. The premise here is that a family—or a system like a community, agency, or organization—is the expert of its own system, knows what is best for it, and benefits from accessing the resources within it or available to it. A major difference between a family and other systems is that one cannot choose the family in which one is born. Other systems, however, can choose who is in or out. This creates an "us" versus "them" mentality, causes polarization, and moves towards social regression. Utilizing the system as a resource is not about exclusion—or about liking everyone within the system—but the system's ability to *function* together, utilizing its resources to better understand members in that system, improve self-regulation, and improve functioning in all life's relationships for all—not just for a few. Note that a family includes those in one's household, households in which one was reared, birth and adopted parents, and/or extended family. Resources can be monetary, knowledge of the systems' history, a particular skill set, connections outside the system, etc.

Helping incorporates key people in the system. This ranges from coaches meeting with several members of one family to gather more information about the family, to ministers staying in ongoing contact with key members in their congregations, to social workers working *with* people in a community to learn what they want, need, and can do to meet their goals. I have worked with families and helpers who have developed a plan based upon what the family wanted and resources they found only to be told no by the court. Helpers from several agencies had worked together to help this family, but no one had been working with the judge. The judge, a key person, was left out of the loop. When helpers and helpees can identify and include key people in the system in the process, they can better enable the family to achieve their goals. As mentioned elsewhere in this book, it is important to "stay connected" to people in the system.

Conclusion

Bowen Theory is not unique in empowering
helpees to problem solve and utilize resources within its
systems nor in encouraging helpers to work on self. Bowen
Theory *is* unique in that it promotes the helper's own work
toward differentiation of self *throughout* the helper's life.
That work lays the foundation for helping others in their
endeavors to do the same. The paradox is that helping is
not always helping. Helping that seeks to tell, dictate,
demand, require, or coerce another does not always help—
nor does coddling. But helping that promotes
differentiation of self from a stance of neutrality and
curiosity so that another can engage their best thinking, see
multigenerational patterns, regulate self, and stay
connected to and utilize the system—this kind of helping
helps. Helping helps when:

- Parents focus on their own functioning in their
  relationships with their family of origin, extended
  family, and spouse/partner instead of their child's
  functioning.
- Clinicians are clear about their availability,
  regardless if their clients liking them or not.
- Ministers explore their struggles with death so they
  can be more present with congregants in their
  grieving process and not use cliches out of their
  own uneasiness.

- Dioceses and denominations utilize their clergy who work day in and out in a community to learn what they think is helpful for that community instead of telling them what to do.
- School administrations lead out of clear principles instead of reacting to parents' reactivity.
- Agencies hire more workers, set more realistic expectations, and promote responsible care and sustainability more than overworking and inadequately training its employees.

As I stated earlier, I do not think my seminary leaders would have said "Go into the world and be a *no* self." The fact that I functioned this way as a young minister came out of my own unresolved emotional process—and was not helpful to others, the congregation, the community, my family, or to me. The paradox is that I can better help another when I do my own work, am clearer and more solid in myself, and utilize my guiding principles, skills, expertise, and experiences to encourage others in their endeavors towards differentiation of self. Fundamental to this is understanding the emotional programming of how I became and function as a helper, when this is a strength, and when it gets in the way of really helping.

Helping is a natural, instinctual reciprocal process that has existed since the beginning of humanity. The helping relationship does not have to be one that is unhelpful; it can be one that promotes better functioning for the helper *and* the helpee, and one that will benefit their families, community, and society in this life and for generations to come.

This chapter represents my observations of what is and is not helpful at this time in my life. I encourage the reader to consider what is and is not helpful. What would the reader add, take away, enhance, etc.? How can the reader change their framework so that helping is less driven by reactivity and unresolved emotional process and more out of ones' own differentiation of self?

NOTES

[1]Boyce, Andy and Dreelin, Andrew. "Ecologists Dig Prairie Dogs, and You Should Too." Smithsonian's National Zoo & Conservation Biology Institute. Jul 02, 2020. https://nationalzoo.si.edu/ conservation-ecology-center/news/ecologists-dig-prairie-dogs-and-you-should-too. MacDonald, D. "Helpers' in Fox Society." *Nature* 282, (1979): 69–71. https://doi.org/10.1038/282069a0. "Naked Mole-rat: Heterocephalus glaber." Sand Diego Zoo. 2003. https://animals.sandiegozoo.org/animals/naked-mole-rat.

[2]Murray Bowen, *Family Therapy in Clinical Practice* (New Jersey: Jarson Aronson, 1985).

[3] Murray Bowen, *The Origins of Family Psychotherapy: The NIMH Family Study Project*. Edited by J. Butler (New York: Jason Aronson, 2013) (emphasis mine), p. 33.

[4]Mary-Frances O'Connor, *The Grieving Brain* (New York: Harper One, 2022), p. 215.

[5]Edwin Friedman, *A Failure of Nerve: Leadership in the Age of the Quick Fix* (New York: Seabury Books, 2007), p. 24.

[6]Walter Smith, "Emotional Cutoff and Family Stability: Child Abuse in Family Emotional Process" in *Emotional Cutoff: Bowen Family Systems Theory Perspectives,* edited by Peter Titelman (New York: The Haworth Clinical Practice Press, 2003), p. 372.

[7]Michael Kerr, *Bowen Theory's Secrets: Revealing the Hidden Life of Families* (New York: W. W. Norton & Company, 2019), p. 95.

[8]Bowen, *Family Therapy in Clinical Practice.*

[9]Bowen, *Family Therapy in Clinical Practice,* p. 541.

[10]Friedman, *A Failure of Nerve: Leadership in the Age of the Quick Fix.*

[11]Robert Noone, *Family and Self: Bowen Theory and the Shaping of Adaptive Capacity* (New York: Lexington Books, 2021), p. 176.

4

Reframing Pastoral Care

James Lamkin

This chapter addresses how Bowen systems theory can help a clergyperson reframe how she or he thinks about the practice of pastoral care. It speaks to the ways a minister can do the work of ministry with greater quality, less stress, and even more fun. Using Bowen Family Systems Theory (BFST), one can see singular occasions in ministry as parts of a systemic whole.

The chapter builds on the writer's experience as a longtime pastor, the reframing discovery of BFST, and what differentiates a systems approach to the practice of ministry. Offered are boots-on-the-ground examples of how the theory might be pastorally implemented, plus the components of a BFST-informed lifelong learning plan for congregational ministers.

The Art of Pastoral Care...A Personal Odyssey

I have been thumbing through a half-century of pastoral care memories. The largest takeaway from this scrapbook review, was my surprise at how much my pastoral theology and practice has changed. Reflection is necessary for awareness and growth. However, the tyranny of the immediate is never far away. A quick scan of the minister's weekly planner includes scheduling baptisms or bar mitzvahs, making hospital visits, preparing sermons, squeezing in funerals, intense committee meetings, and doing the "joyous work" of weddings—all amid the high-maintenance of High Holy Days. This relentless multitude of ministry tasks can take a toll on the *functioning* of a pastor, rector, priest, rabbi, imam, or congregational lay-leader; also, it can blur one's *role* as leader. Overwhelmed, the minister may react by over functioning or under functioning.

A watermark in my own reframing was 1993. Like many ministers, I had tried to read *From Generation to Generation* by Edwin Friedman. It introduced me to BFST. Yet, it was like reading a foreign language. Then, I met Lawrence Matthews, founder of the Leadership in Ministry program. As a clergy coach and in the workshop settings, Larry helped me use the insights of Bowen theory to reframe the terrain of congregational ministry at Ravensworth Baptist Church, Annandale, VA from 1992-

1997, and later at Northside Drive Baptist Church, Atlanta, GA from 1997-2020. Implementing this framework into my pastoral practices, changed my life. I learned to see myself, my family, my vocation, congregations, God, and God's world in life-giving (and even, playful) ways.

The following story is an example of how this "systems epiphany" reframed the way I practice the art of pastoral care.

The Case of the Couple with Cold Feet

A twenty-something man and woman walked with noticeably slow steps across the church parking lot. They were on their way to my study, coming for their third premarital counseling session. They were *not* holding hands.

The bride and groom sat down, glanced around at the walls of books; then, in tandem, breathed a large sigh. The husband-to-be spoke first. "My fiancée and I have discussed our upcoming wedding…and…well…we think we should call it off."

What happened next, was silence.

Like many pastors, I have dabbled in various techniques for premarital counseling. I have given books to read, offered communication instruction, and testing regarding personality and compatibility profiles. But, I've changed.

I now say up-front to a couple, "I would like to have three or four conversations with you as we prepare for your wedding. During these, we will plan the ceremony and talk about your spiritual journeys. Also, I want to know a little about the families in which you grew up. The reason being, *I believe what you bring to a marriage, impacts the marriage more than what happens during the marriage.*"

I go on to say, "As we talk, I will draw a diagram (a genogram) of your family. This will help me remember the names and understand the relationships; and I will show it to you each time we meet."

In the two previous sessions, this couple and I had worked on their family histories. So when the groom, and then the bride, expressed apprehension about marriage commitment, I glanced at their genogram. I suspected that their reluctance about marriage had roots in their family stories. Also, I wondered what relational resources were available to them through their families, which they had not yet claimed and may help.

Eventually, I broke the silence. I turned to the groom and asked, "Have you talked to your father about this ... about your hesitancy?"

He seemed surprised. "No," he said, "talking to my father about this would be difficult."

"Why," I asked?

"Well," said the groom, "he and I just don't talk about such personal things."

Though I did not know the ramifications of what the groom just said, I suspected that we had stumbled upon something important—a significant piece of the emotional process in their relationship.

There's more to tell about the couple with cold feet. They will show up again before the end of the chapter. I have learned that as engaged couples speed *toward* their marriage, part of my job is to invite them to pause and *look back* through the rear-view mirror. I encourage them to explore their family stories which have gotten them to this day. I believe their past has resources they will need.

"I Once Saw…but Now I See…."

As noted, my framework about pastoral care and how I practice it, has changed. I have gotten clearer that the minister's *doing* of pastoral care comes out of the *being* of the minister. I think of the *parson* (a word originally meaning *person*) as the congregational clergy*person* whose first job it is to be emotionally, spiritually, and relationally maturing as a person and as a leader. *Maturity* is *being responsible for one's own emotional and spiritual well-being.* In BFST terms, it means 1) working at your own self-differentiation, 2) while paying attention to staying connected. (These are the law and the prophets of family systems thinking.)[1]

I used to see pastoral caregiving as isolated individual tasks, such as a hospital visits, home visitation, graveside services, or counseling a teenager. However, I now see these ministry occasions as connected. How the pastor lives his or her own life and fulfills his or her vocational responsibilities, carries over into the particular tasks. Births and baptisms and burials are all linked in the pastoral care story arc of the pastor and the parish.

I once thought pastoral care required a particular skill proficiency. Certainly, we could list abilities that help one's functioning, such as listening or clarifying; but I remember rabbi and author Edwin Friedman saying that a focus on technique can raise the anxiety of the minister. It then becomes a skill to "get right." Rather, BFST focuses on functioning in one's *position* within relationships, rather than *techniques* in addressing them. I've learned that to work on my own self, beliefs, and principles is of greater benefit than acquiring certain skills.

I now see the pastor as a general practitioner, not a specialist. Every venue requiring "pastoring" (from individual counseling to preaching) connects to all the other practices. The *parson* brings a *connected, but differentiated presence,* not specialized proficiencies.

Early in my ministry, I functioned like the Lone Ranger. However, the pastor is not a soloist bearing the burden and the blessing of all the pastoral care work. In my first pastorate, I'd never ask a parishioner to go with me on a hospital call or take a deacon with me to visit a widower following a death. But now I do. In other words, I'm always thinking "How might I invite and lead the congregation to share in the work of pastoral care?" The minister is to equip and encourage congregants in ways they can be community; but on the other hand, "...ministry is the work of all the people—not exclusively of the clergy. This requires a refocusing of both the theology and the function of pastoral leadership."[2]

Compare and Contrast: A Pastoral Care Reframing

Pastoral Care has been defined as, "The ministry of the cure of souls, or pastoral care, consists of helping acts, done by representative Christian persons, directed toward the healing, sustaining, guiding, and reconciling of troubled persons whose troubles arise in the context of ultimate meanings and concerns.[3] Also, it "...refers to the solicitous concern expressed within the religious community for persons in trouble or distress."[4]

Another perspective: "In contemporary American usage *pastoral care* usually refers, in a broad and inclusive way, to all pastoral work concerned with the support and nurturance of persons and interpersonal relationships, including everyday expressions of care and concern that may occur in the midst of various pastoring activities and relationships.[5] Each of these carries some truth.

Among traditional pastoral theologians, Seward Hiltner comes closest to my own definition. He laments the narrowing of the focus of pastoral care, while affirming its true breadth. "Indeed, pastoral care has come to be thought of as almost synonymous with pastoral help to the individual person. Such a view forgets that pastoral care has always had a general as well as a special aspect, that is it related *to a group and a congregation* [emphasis mine] as well as to an individual and a family."[6]

Though a bit clunky, I say that reframed pastoral care *is any action taken in relationship with an individual, family, group, or congregation, which is offered by a person connected with a religious tradition, and informed by an appreciation for the connectedness of the faith community.* One could almost say that everything done in and through congregational relationships is some aspect of pastoral care. From the taste of a communion wafer on the Holy Altar held high by an ordained priest, to the flavor of a tuna fish casserole on the kitchen table brought to a grieving household by the Congregational Crisis Committee—pastoral care happens.

Each of the eight concepts of BFST inform a "connected, but differentiated," way of practicing pastoral care. All offer aspects of observing and describing the emotional relationships and processes among families and

family-like groups (such as a congregation). Murray
Bowen said, "The term *emotional* refers to the force that
motivates the system and *relationship* to the ways it is
expressed."[7]

I will briefly mention how four of the concepts relate to
reframing pastoral care.

The Concept of the Emotional Triangle offers an
objective and practical image to describe how anxiety is
handled, and how a third-party is often "used" to stabilize
anxiety. Every minister who has tried to offer pastoral
counseling can relate to this. But the triangle can be a
helpful tool. In the *Cold Footed Couple* story, I used an
existing triangle: 1) The couple's wedding anxiety, 2) the
groom's stuckness, and 3) the resource of the groom's
father. This triangle contained a great deal of energy,
though the father was not in the room.

The Concept of the Differentiation-of-Self
informs that the pastoral leader is a *part of*, but stands *apart
from* all pastoral care situations—from crisis intervention to
routine visitation. Attention to differentiation will help the
minister be aware of the natural impulses of *separateness*
and *togetherness* in all relationships. In the extreme, these
can result in enmeshment (becoming part of the problem)
or being emotionally cut-off (too distant to help).

The Concept of Multigenerational Transmission
is often visible in traditional congregations, some having
four, even five, generations. This makes for the greatest

classroom in the world for a minister who is a student of human behavior. Also, it is a resource in understanding family relationship dynamics that are passed down through generations.

The Concept of Societal Emotional Process may be less visible than other concepts. However, an appreciation for the influences of culture upon the local congregation and denominations is helpful in understanding the ebb and flow of each, as well as the families within them.

The Nuclear Family Emotional System, The Family Projection Process, Emotional Cutoff, and **Sibling Position**. These concepts inform every pastoral care relationship. They assist in observing the variables of anxiety, functioning, and their influence on the capacity for differentiation, both in the congregation and the pastoral caregiver.

Systemic Snapshots: Reframed Pastoral Care Examples

The purpose of these illustrations is to give glimpses into how systems thinking can inform one's pastoral actions.

Pastoral visitation. Lawrence Matthews, the founder of LIM, said, "BFST changed my thinking about ministry. For instance, when a parishioner is in the hospital, I may first visit the patient's family at home. My experience with their family system helps me decide how I offer pastoral care."[9]

During a medical crisis, the pastor may ask himself or herself, "How might I stay connected to the family leader as they make the long journey of transition during this destabilizing time?" This approach can alter, or at least inform, how much time the pastor actually spends beside the hospital bed or in the ICU Waiting Room.

Pastoral Preaching. Fred Craddock said, "Pastoral preaching has…recognized that *the relationship* [emphasis mine] between speaker and listener need not be very different from that between a pastor and a parishioner who has come for counsel. Trust, empathy, and mutuality in strength and weakness, faith and doubt, sin and grace do not destroy the effectiveness of preaching….[and yet] without critical distance, helpfulness dissolves into a pool of pity."[10]

Years ago, I began a Lectionary bible study group in the congregation. Up front, I told them, "I need your help in sermon preparation; and as you help me, you might benefit from in-depth Bible study, as well." It was one of the most lively, playful, and insightful pastoral activities I've done. A dozen people showed-up weekly. One older man frequently told stories about his father and how he viewed the Bible. One woman often told the story, "I could open the door of the house in which I grew up, look into the night sky, and there always was The North

Star, seen through our doorway." (Try to preach on Epiphany and not think of that image). I often asked the group, "How would you say this?" Or, "Let me run this by you." Frequently, they would offer better ideas. During Sunday's sermon, I sometimes referenced the group—often poignantly, also playfully. "I had forgotten that this text is echoed in *Handel's Messiah,* but Amy mentioned that in the Study Group." Or, "I could not find a handle on this text. I asked the Bible study group; and they could not either. However, as we discussed it…there was an ahha!"

Fred Craddock also said, "Sometimes preaching is what the congregation would say if they could." Though discretion and confidentiality always are pastoral values, there are appropriate ways to bring the congregation's voice into the sermon.

Consider: How might the preacher pastorally include the congregation's questions, struggles, hopes, and fears—while being sensitive to confidentiality? Doing so, is an act of differentiation and staying connected.

Pastoral Counseling. This certainly is an organic task in congregational ministry. However, I will leave the heavy lifting to my qualified colleague, Dr. Skip Johnson, in his chapter in this book.

Liturgist. How a worship leader manages himself or herself in the leadership of worship, is a pastoral action. I include it as reframing because it is another place where "self meets self." The parson—at the pulpit, behind the

table, beside the newly baptized, among the pews—
communicates caregiving, conviction, principles, and
values. How one handles oneself, while working on being
a non-anxious presence, when the microphone cuts out or
when the Advent candle doesn't light or when a ten-year-
old throws-up during Palm Sunday's processional (I was a
witness)—builds equity, connection, and credibility in
pastoral relationships.

Celebrant. This includes rituals weddings,
baptisms, and funerals. In *Generation to Generation,* Edwin
Friedman reminds that these rites-of-passage are liminal
times, where, "demons enter and leave the system."[11]
Thus, the parson is attentive to these—as a student and as
a leader.

Regarding funerals, I find it fascinating to observe
which family members attend. Sometimes the uncle who
lives across the street won't come; however, the aunt who
lives in across the country does! I kept a file on every
congregational family. In these I placed correspondence,
parishioner requests ("Sally wants Psalm 23 read at her
funeral."), and notes from pastoral conversations. For
instance, at the graveside service for an 80-year-old father,
I read from a comforting, hand-written letter which the
deceased wrote to me, ten years before, when my own
father died. The reading had a powerful impact on the 55-
year-old son who was sitting on the front row. At the end

of the homily, I gave the letter to him. It was a tangible and meaningful connection.

At a wedding, I held-up a picture which the 25-year-old bride had painted for me, twenty years before when I arrived to pastor the church. In crayon letters it said, "Happy You are Here!" When the attendees saw it, the whole wedding party was ecstatic. They, too, were happy the couple had made it *here* to this moment of celebration; and they were included. I was feeding the newlyweds out of their own basket. Again, this is a reframing because congregational rituals are more than templates and tradition-carriers. They invite parishioners to concentrate the life and love, burdens and blessings—the connections—that already exist within the congregation. However, it often is the relationship and actions of a differentiated pastor which bring these into focus.

Baptism, as practiced by my religious tradition, is believer's baptism. Often this takes place as a young person approaches the teenage years—like a *bar mitzvah*. I always invite the baptismal candidate to write a statement of their own faith, and for them to select someone, perhaps from their family, to read it aloud in worship at the baptism. It is pastoral care work to oversee the confirmand process—but I believe it is vital to the emotional/spiritual process of the confirmand's process of differentiation and connection.

Steward of Simple Routines. This is not a hard-and-fast category. However, I believe it is seminal to the emotional processes with the pastor and congregation. The following are four snippets of how I used simple, easy to manage methods of staying connected to congregants without over functioning.

In the weekly newsletter I occasionally mentioned observable congregational caregiving actions. For example, "The Smith family spoke of their appreciation to our church for the sandwich tray brought by the deacons on the Saturday following Mr. Smith's funeral. This caregiving ministry of the Diaconate, connects the Communion Table in worship with the coffee table of a family in need." The role of the pastoral chronicler is different than that of a historian. Historians report factual events. Chroniclers note the potential meaning of events within a faith community.

I sent weekly *Deacons Plus* emails to all in the congregation who had served as deacons. It was a one-page update regarding non-confidential ministry opportunities; also, shout-outs to the lay ministers. It helped me preemptively alert all of the caregivers of upcoming situations. "As many of you know, Mary W. is now in hospice. Her daughter, Sally, asked for the deacons' prayers during this transition time."

One way to offer connection to peripheral members, was through birthday remembrances. I experimented with form letters, rewritten annually, which also referenced the liturgical seasons of the congregation. I signed each one and wrote a one sentence personal note. E.g. "Fred, I know this is a different kind of birthday and Christmas season for you following Bob's death this past year."

Forty-five years ago, my Clinical Pastoral Education supervisor, Joe Gross, taught me to write down the death date of congregants—and to send the family a note on the anniversary. With digital calendars, it is easy to do; and the remembrance is significant. Following the death of his sister, I wrote a brief letter to the member each year, noting the loss. This simple connection helped change a tense, longtime relationship I had with this church member.

The On-going Opportunities of a Pastoral Care Pedagogy...

Maturity and lifelong learning are vital in ministry. Here are my curriculum suggestions.

1. **Enroll in Leadership in Ministry**.[12] For thirty years, the Leadership in Ministry clergy leadership development program has met twice a year, in various locations, with an experienced faculty. Through plenary presentations and coaching group sessions, participants share case studies from their congregational contexts. In addition, they explore their

families of origin through genograms. Some participants have attended for several years, benefiting from long-term commitment to personal and professional growth.

2. **Work on your genogram as a lifelong project.** Family research builds a capacity to understand and reframe relationships. It can be a resource for how to be present with anxious relationships.

3. **Clarify your personal principles and values.** Let these guide you when anxiety is high. An example is when the congregation is anxious around an issue and the pastor feels pressured to "fix this." Being clear about your principles may help lower you own anxiety as the congregation deals with this issue.

4. **Get a systems savvy ministry coach.** LIM can be a referral source. Rev. Margaret Marcuson is a good example. She is a pastor, author, and experienced systems coach (www.margaretmarcuson.com). Though there are other types of consultants and coaches, I recommend finding a coach who will help you explore your own family history, then connect it with the resources and struggles you currently face.

Oh Yes—The Couple with Cold Feet, Part II....

I doubted that the groom would follow through on my challenge/suggestion to speak with his father. It sounded like an emotional bridge too far; but I was wrong. When the couple returned three weeks later, the groom reported on the conversation, and the wedding was back on! He said the discussion with his father was intimate and honest.

I wasn't much interested in the content of their discussion; but I encouraged and celebrated the "courage of presence" which the groom brought to the process.

So far, they've been married twenty-five years and are the parents of two great kids. My hunch is the groom found something he needed in relationship to his dad that he also needed for his marriage; and, who knows, maybe the father needed it for his marriage, as well.

In Closing…

I believe the local congregation is the nexus for spiritual growth and the epicenter of faith community involvement. This is true in nearly all faith traditions. The reframing of pastoral care offers congregational leaders, lay and clergy, a way of seeing emotional process that is vigorous and vital.

Perhaps the reader can take these thoughts of separateness and togetherness, differentiated yet connected, plus the ongoing work of lowering one's anxiety—and translate them to his or her own faith tradition context. As Edwin Friedman often said, "This theory only applies to all protoplasm on the planet."

NOTES

[1]Edwin H. Friedman, *Generation to Generation: Family Process in Church and Synagogue* (New York, Guilford Press, 1985), p. 229. Friedman also underscored these two values in many of his presentations.

[2]Israel Galindo, *The Hidden Lives of Congregations,* (Herndon, VA, The Alban Institute, 2004), p. 194.

[3]William A. Clebsch and Charles R. Jaekle, *Pastoral Care in Historical Perspective,* (Englewood Cliffs, NY, Prentice-Hall, 1964) p. 4.

[4]L.O. Mills, "Pastoral Care (History, Traditions, and Definitions)," in *Dictionary of Pastoral Care and Counseling,* ed. Rodney J. Hunter, (Nashville, Abingdon Press, 1990) pp. 836-7.

[5]L.O. Mills, "Pastoral Care (History, Traditions, and Definitions)," p. 845.

[6]Steward Hiltner, *Preface to Pastoral Theology,* (Nashville, Abingdon Press, 1958) p. 216.

[7]Murray Bowen, *Family Therapy in Clinical Practice,* (N.J., Jason Aronson, 1978), p. 158.

[8]*The Bowen Center for the Study of the Family* website: Learn about Bowen Theory. The Bowen Center for the Study of the Family, February 4, 2023.

[9]From a presentation by Larry Matthews, during a Leadership in Ministry workshop, at Lost River Retreat Center, Lost River, WV, March 1993.

[10]Fred Craddock, "Pastoral Preaching," in *Dictionary of Pastoral Care and Counseling,* ed. Rodney J. Hunter, (Nashville, Abingdon Press, 1990) pp. 944.

[11]Edwin H. Friedman, "A Family Approach to Life-Cycle Ceremonies," *Generation to Generation: Family Process in Church and Synagogue* (New York, Guilford Press, 1985), p. 162.

[12] Leadership in Ministry is part of the Pastoral Excellence Program at the Center for Lifelong Learning, Columbia Theological Seminary, Decatur, GA (www.ctsnet.edu).

5

Reframing Pastoral Counseling: Abiding

Skip Johnson

I have always considered pastoral counseling to be a specialized sub-category of professional ministry that can be located within the broad framework of pastoral care. It exists as one area of a multi-faceted ministerial vocation. For my purposes pastoral care can be understood as a disposition of the mind, heart, and spirit applicable to all pastoral interactions, an approach of solicitous concern lending a distinctive tone to a host of ministerial actions from administration to worship.

Pastoral counseling becomes a distinctive expression of pastoral care by being more formal and structured in its operation, as well as being informed by a theory of practice that organizes its performance from initiation to termination. Pastoral care occurs within every ministerial encounter: the chance meeting at the grocery store, the greeting of parishioners before a worship service, the visitation in the hospital room. Pastoral counseling by contrast functions out of a mutually consented and contractual agreement between parties in distress and a counseling pastor. It is established in pursuit of a purposeful agenda for the work of personal healing, liberation and reconciliation, both emotional and spiritual.

I have practiced as a pastoral counselor for approximately 40 years. I've served as the clinical director of a training program for a well-regarded pastoral counseling center. I've also taught seminary and graduate courses in pastoral care theory and served local congregations as an ordained minister under appointment within the United Methodist denomination. Gazing backward from this vantage, I recognize that my pastoral counseling work over the years was shaped by the prevailing cultural and clinical winds that emerged from a narrow selection of conceptual theories, each of them heralded and touted by a variety of Western-oriented higher education sources, researchers and continuing education programs.

For me professionally, object relations, relational psychoanalytic frameworks, Jungian and existential/humanistic approaches have all demonstrated their usefulness for conceptualizing the inward experiences of hurting individuals. They have each offered me a place to stand so that I might thoughtfully approach the mystery of the causal factors that have brought others existential pain.

They have provided me with effective strategies for healing interventions, collaboration and growth.

Over the last ten years family systems theory, stemming from the work of Murry Bowen in the 1960's, has also begun to offer a useful reframing of pastoral counseling that I believe will be with me for a while. It has intrigued me with its expressed leanings toward a biological-based beginning point and its provision of a comprehensive theory of human existence both separate and in relationship.

Our evolution as living creatures over hundreds of thousands of years has resulted in patterned ways for our brains to address the anxiety that accompanies all life. An appreciation of the Bowenian concepts used in systems theory can assist, illuminate, and reframe the care we seek as pastors to offer to others. Given an invitation to reflect on the usefulness of Bowen's theory for pastoral counseling leads me toward these brief reflections.

In my teaching and my counseling practice, as well as in my ministry work serving congregations, I have found myself increasingly thinking about the persons with whom I sit as men and women with whom I will do my best to "abide." I am using the word in both a theological and practical manner. As pastors we know the word from the Gospel of John, in which the word suggests an active closeness. We are also familiar with the word from the Henry Lyte hymn, "Abide With Me." The hymn's first verse captures the yearning of hurting souls for a presence willing to witness to their pain. The word itself comes from an Old English root meaning; to endure, sustain, to bear, and to remain in service of. More expansive definitions recognize that to abide with another is to commit to a time of journeying together, to dwell alongside.

Central to Bowen systems theory is an appreciation of personal boundaries. We exist in a swirl of relationships that overlap. To abide in a caring and professional way with another implicitly acknowledges someone else's story as theirs and not ours. An abiding counselor comes along side but does not overstep. They are intentionally connected but not overwhelmed to the point they become enmeshed participants with another's emotional struggle.

Abiding requires a self-reflective and active respect for the existence of the other as an autonomous being. It also demands a personal commitment to doing the work necessary to keep oneself clear and separate from embracing responsibility for the actions, feelings and outcome of another's life. Their journey is not mine to impose upon. Their salvation must be personally claimed. It is not something I can grant, gift, or graft.

A broad overarching goal behind all pastoral counseling from a Bowenian systems framework is to assist the other to learn to "abide" themselves as a distinct self within the various emotional systems in which they are participants. We are all committed and connected to

others. We need relationships. But we must take care that
we do not become fused with another in a blurry
confusion of overlapping self-experience. I will offer my
best clinical tools as I abide with you and will listen deeply
with compassion, but I bring harm and hubris if I overstep
and attempt to repair and take responsibility for your life
journey.

Thinking about "ABIDE" as a metaphor invites me
to a playful exercise of considering the word itself as an
acronym sketching out pastoral counseling from a systems
framework. I offer this not as an exhaustive recipe but as
an imaginative guide assisting our orientation for this
work of thoughtful care.

Acceptance

"*A*" reminds us of the *acceptance* of the other as
they present themselves at this particular point in their
lives and ours, along with our *acceptance* of a willingness to
set aside the required time, energy and conditions needed
for appropriate listening and responding. It carries with it
the purposeful bracketing of distractions that would draw
one's *attention* to other directions and *acknowledges* making
the necessary conscious decision to open oneself to the
counselee's story. Good listening, genuine *abiding*, takes
purposeful energy. It is not easy. With *acceptance* comes a

readiness to make room for the other and a willingness to be an *active* participatory witness to their struggle.

The *"A"* of ABIDE also includes an understanding of *anxiety* as an ever-present emotional field within the self that must be carefully regulated as a part of daily life. The gift of living generates anxiety as a felt background alertness, an awareness that can be a low hum held and contained or an enormity of emotional reverberation that can surge to debilitating levels that can flood, distort, and severely limit our abilities. Our response to the experience of *anxiety* can bind or loosen a capacity for thoughtful engagement, for responding to a level of reactivity with another's interior and exterior world, as well as monitoring this within ourselves.

Elevated *anxiety* diminishes *agency*, our ability to act with intentionality and meaningful purpose in our lives. Anxiety can also become viral and spread from one individual to another. Its amplification is capable of distorting rational thinking and stifling creativity, leading to reactivity over responsiveness, regression over adaptation. It can lead to what has been described as an "amygdala hijack" as the brain is overwhelmed with feelings and falls into a flight, fight, or freeze response. Yet anxiety can also be dampened and its level lowered by attention to functional facts or by meditative practice. It should always be the aspirational maxim of the pastoral counselor to strive to be the least anxious person in the room and they should have in their professional and personal toolbox proven methods readily available that can allow them to off load their own anxiety in order to function in their role as a pastoral counselor.

Boundaries

The "*B*" in ABIDE signifies an appreciation and respect of the *boundaries* necessary to promote the development of a self, that essence of personal identity able to grow, act, and love with meaningful intent. Bowen's theory emphasizes how thinking clearly and receiving guidance in decision making from established principles reinforces boundaries of the self. Strong, intense feelings can dissolve them and lead to enmeshment, a blurring of the lines that separate you from others, resulting in an emotional fusion where it becomes difficult to separate an "I" from a "we." One of the easiest and clearest declaration of boundaries comes with the use of the "I" statement to own one's intent and experience, along with a healthy ability to offer an appropriate "No" when necessary. Boundaries define and inform us so that we might affirm, this is who we are.

Another "*B*" word is the concept of "*binding*," a suspension and holding of personal anxiety preventing its leakage into decision making and action. Anxiety can be bound by firm principles and tethered by strong beliefs.

Trusting relationships offer a containment field to prevent anxiety from becoming overwhelming and from dissolving the boundaries that allow us to function as independent persons. Faith stories and scripture can also serve to bind anxiety.

Intergenerational

The letter *"I"* brings to mind several key terms applicable for a pastoral counseling practice informed by systems theory. *Intergenerational* reminds the counselor that experienced anxiety patterns can be traced backward over time by an engagement with the counselee's family history, a history that can be explored with the use of genograms and storytelling. Long standing patterns that have been operational in the lives of parents, grandparents and previous generations are brought to light through conversation to the reflective and conscious foreground of the present. Once rendered visible in the present they provide lenses through which to understand both adaptive and maladaptive coping behaviors that have been active for generations and have become stealth strategies for balancing a homogeneity within an experience of anxiety.

Integrity is another **"I"** word. It underscores the robustness of the boundaries surrounding the counseling and how it needs to be conducted. This begins with confidentiality and basic respect for the work but also implies a principled approach to pastoral counseling from a beginning point of sound theory and understanding.

I consider *imagination* to be a key "I" term. The counselee can only be encountered as an "other," the story of their pain and struggle is only available through what I term the activity of compassionate *imagination* in the counselor. It is through the use of our *imagination* that we are able to comprehend how others have adapted themselves to their world. It is also through *imagination* that our mind fashions its tools of counseling practice and applies them to another's situation.

Differentiation

"**D**" links the practitioner of a systems informed pastoral counseling practice to the Bowenian concept of *differentiation*, that ability to privilege thinking over feeling. The goal of life from a Bowenian framework is the ongoing flourishing of an authentic self, not so much a destination to be reached as a dynamic awareness and balance to be lived into over a lifetime in the presence of fluctuating anxiety. Differentiation is a process of emergence occurring over one's entire life span requiring continual integration of new facts and circumstances, additions and losses, as well as a constant interplay with a balance of internal anxiety.

Empathy

"**E**" brings to mind the word *empathy* which I define as compassionate imagination. This is not sympathetic understanding envisioned within the frame of our personal history but an active imagined rendering of the other's experience inviting them to share their frame. *Emotional* process is a phrase meant to capture the sense of all of human life as caught up in ongoing exchanges of information both emotional and factual, verbal and non-verbal. We are all connected and impact each other. There is no exception to this. We create shared emotional systems "whenever two or more are gathered."

I want to close with an affirmation that a basic need of human life lies with finding others who can bear witness to our pain as well as to our triumphs. We are made for relationships. We connect to others through our vulnerabilities, not our strengths. The preacher's call from a pulpit, "can I have a witness," is an existential cry for life's wounds to be heard and acknowledged. To **abide** with another answers that cry and carries it a further step. Not only do I hear you, but I will also stand beside you in the midst of this period of shadow, because as the hymn tells us "fast falls the eventide" and "the darkness deepens." To do this work well is to offer a gift of grace that blesses both parties while respecting our bounded selves.

6

Reframing the Role of the Coach

Meg Hess and Margaret Marcuson

In this chapter we explore how coaching is understood and utilized in the context of The Leadership in Ministry Workshops (LIM). Addressing both formal and informal coaching, we describe what a coach does in Bowen Family Systems Theory (BFST) coaching, name some potential pitfalls, and identify the internal work that is required of the coach.

What is coaching in the light of BFST?

The International Coaching Federation (ICF) defines coaching as "...partnering with clients in a thought-provoking and creative process that inspires them to maximize their personal and professional potential."[1] The emphasis here is on the collaborative nature of the coaching relationship. The Coach assumes the client to be "creative, resourceful, and whole" and accompanies them as they identify and access their resources, strengths, and abilities while moving toward their ministry goals.

The coaching approach in LIM is what we call "content rich coaching." One of the goals for participants is to learn and apply the theory both personally and professionally. Teaching the theory is assumed to be a part of every coaching agenda in both individual and group sessions. Plenary sessions teach about the eight main concepts of BFST: Differentiation of Self, Nuclear Family Emotional Process, Family Projection Process, Triangles, Multigenerational Transmission Process, Emotional Cut-off, Sibling Position, and Societal Emotional Process.

Group coaching includes individual genogram work as participants explore their family of origin story. Identifying unresolved family of origin issues, noting family patterns, tracing the family's level of chronic anxiety, and identifying family strengths and resources are some elements of genogram research. Participants also apply the theory as they present congregational case studies to their coaching groups. Whether presenting their own material or listening to others present, everyone is learning to "think theory."

Participants begin this learning process before the gathering as they prepare their genograms and congregational case studies for presentation. The learning continues between sessions as LIM participants take on research projects, where they pay close attention to observing what they are learning about themselves as they try out new strategies and approaches to ministry. For example, by observing the nuances of how they react to increased anxiety in the system they develop better skills at self-regulation and less reactive functioning as a leader. This action-reflection model contributes to the coaching goal of increased self-awareness.

What does a coach do from the perspective of BFST?

Overall, the Bowen-oriented coach's primary work is to be present as a differentiated, curious self and to foster differentiation in others. What does differentiation mean? "A person with a well-differentiated 'self' recognizes his realistic dependence on others, but he can stay calm and clear headed enough in the face of conflict, criticism, and rejection to distinguish thinking rooted in a careful assessment of the facts from thinking clouded by emotionality. Thoughtfully acquired principles help guide decision-making about important family and social issues, making him less at the mercy of the feelings of the moment."[2] The coach encourages the coachee to get clear about their own principles, to see their agency in the dilemmas at hand, and to work on their part in difficult relationships, both in the ministry setting and in their family of origin. This is most effective in a coaching relationship over time. Leadership in Ministry workshop participants return year after year to take part in a process that helps them be more thoughtful in all their relationships.

Powerful questions are a fundamental coaching tool use in the workshops. These are open-ended questions that invite the coachee to draw on their own wisdom, strengths, and resources as they think through the application of BFST. The goal is to help the coachee "get up in the balcony" — to shift their framework — and examine their functioning as leaders within the dynamics of a system. We have included a list of sample questions that reflect the concepts of the theory at the end of the chapter. In addition to providing ample opportunities for the coachee to reflect, questions of curiosity are also a way for the coach to maintain appropriate distance from the coachee and give them space to do their own thinking.

Emotional Triangles in the Coaching Relationship

Every coaching relationship includes multiple relationship (emotional) triangles. Managing self in these triangles is a critical part of the coaching process. A triangle is a "three-person relationship system. It is considered the building block or 'molecule' of larger emotional systems because a triangle is the smallest stable relationship system. A two-person system is unstable because it tolerates little tension before involving a third person…. If the tension gets too high for one triangle to contain it spreads to a series of 'interlocking' triangles."[3]

One method is having the coachee diagram the triangles to visualize emotional process. Depicting interlocking triangles is at the heart of the diagramming process and critical to the coaching work. The coach engages in triangles presented in the coaching in a neutral way. The coach is present with the coachee, but does not take the coachee's side in the case study being presented. Instead, diagramming helps the coachee reflect on the relationship processes at work with more neutrality.

Triangles are presented as neutral: "Bowen researchers consider triangles a natural function of living systems. Triangles can have either negative or positive outcomes depending on how their members manage anxiety and reactivity. Bowen postulated that if one member of the triangle remains calm and in emotional contact with the other two, the system automatically calms down."[4] Supporting the coachee through the process of diagramming is one example of content-rich coaching where instruction and guidance takes place.

Coaching work requires that the coach remains calm and in contact with the coachee. The coach encourages participants to calmly think through how to connect with the other two sides of the triangle.

In the Leadership in Ministry workshop and other BFST-oriented coaching sessions, the genogram or family diagram is a useful tool to help the coachee reflect on the family of origin processes which may contribute to both stuckness and strength in handling challenges. Questions about the "who," "what," "when," and "where," of the family history help the coachee get curious about their family story and can lead to a new perspective on the family. The focus on facts of the family is essential. This approach discourages "Why" questions, since no one can realistically fully know the motivations of others, in the present and certainly not in the past. The diagram can also be used as an adjunct to work on specific ministry challenges, to see where the family story may provide clues to the coachee's difficulty in managing relationships—or to family strengths that could contribute to a new framework and approach.

At the end of the coaching session, the coachee is invited to identify what they are taking away from the experience. Inviting them to think about what will help them remember what they have discovered and identifying next steps or strategies for further integration of the theory keeps the intersection of theory and practice front and center. Knowing that they will be reporting back to the group in the future strengthens the value of accountability in coaching.

What is the internal work required of a coach using BFST to avoid common coaching pitfalls?

The differentiated presence, more than the best questions or any other coaching technique, is what creates space for change. As Rabbi Edwin Friedman used to say, "What you bring is not technique, but the nature of your presence." This means that the more self-aware coaches are, and the more they have worked on the challenging relationships in their family of origin, the freer they will be in all relationships, including the coaching relationship. They will be clearer about their own principles and practices, and less likely to get caught up in taking responsibility for coachees. The rich tapestry of coaching is strengthened by the addition of BFST to the coaching model.

It's easy in coaching to take on the anxiety of the coachee facing a challenging circumstance. The differentiating work of the coach is to allow the coachee to sit with their challenge in a space that helps them think about it and not simply react. The coach may suggest ideas, but leaves room for the coachee to accept them or not. The coach also challenges coachees to think for themselves about their dilemmas, options and opportunities for growth.

One of the biggest pitfalls for coaches is to feel overly responsible for coachees and their dilemmas. This can show up in advice giving or simply talking too much. One way to stay out of pressuring the coachee to accept your ideas is to wonder with the coachee about options-- inviting the coachee to generate ideas for themself and to offer, and, in a light way, offer an idea or two. The work is to have little investment in whether or not they take you up on the idea. The coach does not want the coachee to be too dependent on them or their ideas.

A basic principle is this: The coach should not be working harder than the coachee. I (MJM) find that if I'm tired after a coaching session, I've been working too hard. When a coach is working with someone who has entered coaching because they've been assigned, for example, it can be easy to get caught in trying to motivate them. My first coach in Edwin Friedman's training program, Lee Gruber, used to say a mentor of hers would recommend, "Feel the back of your chair." Sometimes I literally lean back in my chair to let my body remind me not to be engaged in ways that don't help the client.

An additional pitfall can be to try to convince people of the value of Bowen theory and this approach to thinking about ministry. One way to stay out of that is simply to mention elements of theory in a neutral way. In content-rich coaching, the end goal is not mere learning of theory but better functioning.

Another challenge for the coach is to remain clear about their role and function. Effective coaching requires that the coach define and stay in the coaching role. The coach is not a consultant, who offers ideas, strategies, and solutions in the service of problem solving. The coach is not a psychotherapist, who makes a diagnosis and creates a treatment plan. The coach is not a mentor who dispenses wisdom and knowledge. Although certain aspects of these roles may be present to some degree in coaching, the primary role is to help "...unlock previously untapped sources of imagination, productivity, and leadership." (ICF website). Staying in the role of the coach means consistently inviting the ministerial leader to develop their own thinking about what leadership is according to the BFST model.

The internal challenge for the coach includes doing your own work and knowing your own emotional hot spots. A BFST-oriented coach prepares by getting their own coaching around their family of origin, preparing a family genogram and doing the work of beginning to differentiate a self within that family. It's important to understand your own family of origin, and to continue to reference your own genogram as a working document. For example, my family of origin (MJM) is full of older sisters and younger brothers. I'm the oldest daughter of an oldest daughter who was a pastor's daughter. I can get caught in being annoyed with an underfunctioning male coachee or trying too hard with them. By contrast, coach and family therapist and LIM faculty member Elaine Boomer talks about growing up as her father's favorite, with emotional distance from her mother. She has to work not to give men an extra break.

Conclusion

Many skills from mainstream models of coaching are useful in BFST coaching. Deep listening, cultivating presence, identifying the agenda, working with the coachee's strengths, using metaview to get a bigger picture, intruding and interrupting, and knowing when silence is an improvement over speech are a few of those skills that we use when coaching ministerial leaders. The framework of a coaching session that begins with clarifying the agenda of the session and ends with accountability around next steps is a helpful structure for BFST coaching.

One of the unique features of our approach to coaching is the use of the concepts of BFST as a theory of practice for ministry. Coaching in this context is a learning lab for differentiating a Self in leadership. The framework of BFST helps the coach to navigate the potential pitfalls in coaching. When the coach does the internal work of self-regulating while staying within the perimeters of the coaching role they model differentiation of self in a helping role. It would be easy in this model to over focus on giving the coachee an explanation of the theory by

"Bowen 'splaining." Yet the strength in this model lies in its ability to give both coach and coachee not just the theory but also the experience of thoughtful, principled leadership in practice.

NOTES:

[1]See the ICF website: https://coachingfederation.org/

[2]Michael Kerr, *One Family's Story: A Primer on Bowen Theory* (Georgetown Family Center, 2017).

[3]Kerr, *One Family's Story.*

[4]See the Vermont Center for Family Studies website. https://vermontcenterforfamilystudies.org/about/bowen-family-systems-theory

Coaching Questions Using the
Eight Concepts of Bowen Theory

Differentiation of Self

- What is your role as a leader here?
- Who in the system is most motivated to change?
- How might you invite people to take responsibility for themselves?
- What is your thinking about this issue? Your beliefs? Your feelings?
- How might you self-regulate more effectively in this situation?
- What is your understanding of effective leadership?
- What is your understanding of healthy leadership?
- What are your resources for self-regulation and self-care?
- How do you get clear about _____ within yourself?
- How do you stay connected with those on the opposite side of an issue?
- What gets in the way of your being curious?
- What research projects in your own family can help you be more thoughtful about this issue in your ministry setting?
- How do you know when you are anxious?
- How do you know when you are being reactive?
- Are there resources in your family of origin that you can consult for guidance on this issue?

- Who does that person remind you of in your family?
- What is your family motto?
- How are you likely to be seduced?
- How are you likely to flame out?
- What do you want?

Nuclear Family Emotional Process
- Where does elevated anxiety usually show up in this system?
- What was your role in your family of origin re: anxiety? (Generator, Amplifier,
- Absorber, Distributer, providing calm, thoughtful leadership)
- Why now?
- What do you think about the timing of this conflict?
- What function does the conflict serve in the system? Regulating closeness/distance?
- Where do you see sabotage at play in the System?
- What are the primary stressors at work in this System?
- How do you know when you are over-functioning? Under-functioning?
- What do you know about the family of origin of this individual?
- Who are you pursuing? Who is coming toward you? Who are you avoiding?

Family Projection Process

- Do you notice any patterns in how the anxiety is being distributed throughout the System?
- Who is the symptom bearer or identified patient in the system? Have they played that role before?
- Who in your family ordained you?

Triangles

- Can you draw the main triangles in this case study? Where are you in each of these triangles?
- Are you on the inside or the outside of this triangle?
- How might you take a more neutral position in this triangle? What would that look like?
- How do you know when you're in the "burn-out position" in a triangle?
- Whose anxiety are you holding in this triangle? For the System?
- How might you hand the anxiety back to where it belongs?
- What structural groups/individuals might you triangle in to help address this issue? (Boards, committees, leaders, *denominational resources*, etc.)
- What was your position in the primary triangle in your family of origin?

Multigenerational Transmission Process

- What are the strengths/weaknesses that are present in the DNA of this system?
- How have the last five leaders left the System?
- Are there patterns of reactivity in this system?
- What do you know about the history of this dynamic in this congregation?
- What is the history of the people who have held this position? How have they functioned?

Emotional Cut-off

- What is the history of people leaving the congregation? What have been the issues cited?
- Are there any splits in the history?

Sibling Position

- What was your sibling position in your FOO? How might those old patterns of functioning be showing up here? How might you function differently?
- What are the sibling positions of the key players in this situation?

Societal Emotional Process

- How might Societal anxiety be showing up in your setting?
- Is there anything going on in the wider denomination that might affect this situation?

7

Reframing Interim Ministry: Becoming a "Real" Pastor. A Report from the Laboratory of Church Leadership Transition

Joel Alvis

The first Sunday of my new call as interim pastor of a mid-sized suburban congregation had gone well. I shared who I was and what I hoped to help them accomplish in this time of transition. I invited folks to let me know their concerns and issues. One couple approached me while I was greeting people at the sanctuary entrance. She had a scowl on her face and he a grimace. She said: *"You better not be like the interim from hell we had at our last church!"*

Ask any group of church people: *What kind of experience have you had during a time of "interim" ministry?* there will be all sorts of responses. Some experience a time as a positive change. Others, as the woman above, describe it as, well, as *hell*. Some are so glad that the previous pastor is gone that they cannot contain themselves. Others are still grieving the departure of the pastor who founded the congregation; or conducted their wedding; or baptized their children; or buried their parent or spouse; or helped them through a life crisis. Some will measure a new pastor against what they think the former pastor did (or did not do).

I served in interim and transitional roles for fifteen years. Loren Mead and the Alban Institute laid the foundations for what became known as "interim" ministry in the 1960s and 1970s. In more recent times, "transitional" has come to be used in place of "interim" to describe this type of in-between ministry. The terms may be used interchangeably.[1]

A Real Pastor?

On one occasion early in my sojourn, the church was interviewing seminary students for an internship. One candidate asked me during the course of our conversation: "So when are you going to be a real pastor again?" The implication being that transitional pastors are not "real" pastors. Some view transitional ministry as a kind of jobs programs for pastors who hit a rough patch or could not be a "real" pastor. Some view the task of ministry between installed (or settled) pastors as just keeping the lights on. A Presbytery leader once said he categorically believed that during times of pastoral transition congregations lose money, momentum and membership because a "real" pastor" was not present.

What does it mean to be a "real" pastor?

That question brings to mind the famous children's story of *The Velveteen Rabbit* by Margery Williams. A toy rabbit made of velveteen is brought to the nursery. The other toys counsel the young rabbit on what awaits. The premise of the story is that reality comes from relationship.

Real isn't how you are made,' said the Skin Horse. 'It's a thing that happens to you. When a child loves you for a long, long time, not just to play with, but REALLY loves you, then you become Real.'

'Does it hurt?' asked the Rabbit.

'Sometimes,' said the Skin Horse, for he was always truthful. 'When you are Real you don't mind being hurt.'

'Does it happen all at once, like being wound up,' he asked, 'or bit by bit?'

'It doesn't happen all at once,' said the Skin Horse. 'You become. It takes a long time. That's why it doesn't happen often to people who break easily, or have sharp edges, or who have to be carefully kept. Generally, by the time you are Real, most of your hair has been loved off, and your eyes drop out and you get loose in the joints and very shabby. But these things don't matter at

*all, because once you are Real you can't be ugly, except to people
who don't understand."* [2]

Becoming a "real" pastor involves walking with
people, individually and with congregations, through
difficult times and places in their lives. Some speak of it as
"being there."

Another way of speaking about becoming "real" is
through the language of Bowen Family System Theory.
Developed by psychiatrist Murray Bowen and brought to
congregational leaders through the work of Edwin
Friedman and others, this theory posits several concepts
about the self and the relation of self to the world.

The key to maintaining the balance of self and
connection with the rest of the world is the concept of
Differentiation of Self. Edwin Friedman described
differentiation as "*. . .the capacity to become one's self out of
one's self with minimum reactivity to the positions or reactivity
of others. Differentiation is charting one's own way by means of
one's own internal guidance system, rather than perpetually
eyeing the 'scope' to see where others are at."*

A summary phrase from *A Failure of Nerve* about
differentiation is, it "*. . . refers to a direction in life rather than
a state of being."* Friedman goes on to emphasize that the
concept of differentiation is not about behavior. It is about
"*. . . the fabric of one's existence, one's integrity."* [3]

Different faith traditions have different ways of
defining who a pastor is and what a pastor does. Query a

group of pastors what their function and role is, and no doubt, you will receive more answers than the number of people asked. In general, a pastor is a leader responsible to a group of people, who preaches and teaches from the community's sacred texts, offers sacraments, provides appropriate spiritual guidance, and helps a community of the faithful organize itself to live out its calling.[4]

The practice in churches through the years has been to be served by pastors recognized, affirmed, and trained for that calling. That has been one of the functions that denominations provided. They have a process of credentialing individuals who complete a set of requirements to be set apart (ordained) as a spiritual leader.

There comes a time when a pastor needs to leave a congregation. Sometimes it is because of another call to ministry. Sometimes it is because the pastor and/or the congregation have grown to arrive in different places. Maybe it is because of some malfeasance that was identified. Sometimes it is because the pastor retires. Or dies. There are many reasons that pastoral tenures come to an end. But they all do at some point.

No American pulpiteer and theologian may be as notable as Jonathan Edwards. Yet Edwards' ministry in Northampton, Massachusetts ended in conflict in 1751. Edwards left for another pulpit and then to become president of the College of New Jersey, later known as

Princeton. While there is much scholarship about the preacher, theologian, and leader that Edwards was, there are not many references to the impact of the conflict on the Northampton congregation. [5]

Pastoral leadership transitions in congregations has a long history. The *New York Times* of March 4, 1888 reprinted an item from the *Boston Journal* of a day earlier noting: *There is an unusually large number of vacant pulpits in Boston at present.* The item listed the need for pastoral leaders in six Congregational churches, two Universalists churches, two Baptists churches, and one church each for the Unitarians, Presbyterians and Episcopalians. [6]

The term used historically to describe this in between period in a church's life is "vacancy." This derives from the idea that if a position, such as pastor, is not being occupied, it is "vacant." This is an archaic use, yet one which still crops up once in a while.

After completing the Harry Potter series, J. K. Rowling's first novel was *The Casual Vacancy.* It tells the tale of what happens in a small English town when a member of the town council dies unexpectedly. There is a rush to fill the vacancy and much scheming among town folk. As events unfold two citizens realize something about this "opportunity": "... *they ...were contemplating the casual vacancy; and they saw it, not as an empty space but as a magician's pocket full of possibilities*" [7]

Some see pastoral transition as a time to scheme. Others find in them possibilities for pursuing new pathways. No matter how it is handled, a pastoral transition is a time of anxiety in a congregation.

The Installed or Settled Pastor

Different traditions use the word installed or settled pastorates to describe a pastor whose call is not bound by time. The role of one who serves as pastor in between installed pastors is defined by time. An installed pastor begins with no end date in mind. Interim or transitional ministry assumes an end time.

Often, but not always, the pastor in this in-between time agrees to not be a candidate for the permanent position. The times allowed for this work vary depending on the way the congregation operates by its polity and policy. In all times of transition, there is a desire to move beyond the present moment to some future state. So, what happens in this time in between?

In his groundbreaking book *A Change of Pastors,* Loren Mead argued that change is possible in congregations during transitions unlike at any other time. It is at such moments that the status quo (or, homeostasis in Bowen Theory language) is vulnerable. Mead wrote that the transition is a time when the status quo "*. . . can be questioned and explored without a sense of obligation."* In fact,

Mead claimed the impact of pastoral changes are the biggest change events in any congregation's life. [8]

A New Framework

Bowen Family System Theory provides a new framework for understanding the function of a leader in the system. So, what happens when the person in leadership changes? Each person who serves any given church as pastor will fulfill the leadership function in their own ways. Edwin Friedman pointed this out when he noted: *"A problem common to all systems theory: How to account for change at all if systems are perpetually kept in balance by their own homeostatic forces."*[9]

Transition is a process, not a person. Sometimes in church life the person who is the pastor during the transitional period is called The Interim. Sometimes the expectation is that the interim pastoral leader is to do all the work. The work of interim ministry, however, as is all ministry, resides in the life of the congregation. The task of the pastoral leader in these times is to shepherd the congregation to the next place of ministry.

Transition does not begin on a specific date. Anxiety is always present and manifest itself in different ways. One technique to picture this in a congregational setting is the Johari Window. [10]

The Johari Window

	Known to self	Not known to self
Known to others	Arena	Blind Spot
Not Known to others	Façade	Unknown

The window illustrates that there are things known and things unknown in the life of both a pastor and a congregation. The intersections of the matters known and unknown and by whom are places where anxiety may appear.

For example, when a pastor is approaching retirement age, the congregation will notice how the pastor conducts herself or himself. If the pastor continues to serve without fully declaring their intentions, side conversations among lay leaders and members will begin. Or when a pastor completes a major milestone in ministry—the completion of a building or receiving a degree, or at a time of personal change, the birth of a child or a marriage or divorce—the pastor often becomes open to receive another call. The very act of being open and then circulating that interest requires energy and effort that takes away from the focus on congregational issues. In other cases, a group within the church can decide that a pastor is no longer needed and set in motion events that result in a departure. Such behavior also generates anxiety.

Some pastors approaching retirement are reticent to discuss their plans. Nor do pastors seeking another call share this intention with their congregations. And conflict can be a significant factor in church life contributing to anxiety. Not every occasion of such events results in a pastoral departure. Yet when the time comes for a dissolution of a pastoral relationship there is always a trail for anyone interested in identifying it.

For example, I served as an interim pastor after the retirement of the founding pastor with more than thirty years ministry. He declared his intention to retire at the beginning of a year with the plan that a transition would be well underway when he left. As I listened to congregational leaders, they had been aware for several years that the retirement was in the works but did not question his timeline. This pastor was deeply admired by the congregation. Despite the anxiety and uncertainty present, meaningful ministry was still accomplished during the last years of his tenure. But as time moved forward there was increased anxiety and uncertainty as the congregation wrestled with the realities of moving forward to the next pastoral leader.

In another instance, I followed a pastor who departed in the midst of a conflict over the denominational identity of the congregation. Within a few months of his departure he had become pastor of a new congregation founded by former members in another denomination.

Members who remained in the church were distraught, disturbed, and angry by these events. Despite losing several significant families who accounted for a sizeable portion of donations, others who had not been giving at a robust level stepped forward. While there was a net decrease in giving, the ministry of the church continued with some modifications. When the pressing need for renovations of the sanctuary's stained-glass windows was acknowledged, a mini-capital funds campaign was oversubscribed for the necessary restoration.

Pastoral leadership transition occurs in the midst of culture and change at the congregational, denominational, and personal level. Navigating these challenges is to live through anxious times.

The Emergence of Interim Ministry

Since Loren Mead pioneered the calling of "interim" ministry, special training has been developed. Several denominations have their specialized cohorts of pastors for such callings. The Interim Ministry Network emerged from this emphasis and includes numerous denominational cohorts. But the legacy of Bowen Family System Theory is a feature you can find in many training programs.

For example, the introduction to training of the Interim Ministry Network is:

Foundations of Transitional Ministry. Using General Systems Theory, Bowen Family Systems Theory and William Bridges' Theory on Change and Transition, attendees explore the unique dynamics of congregations in transition and understand how a congregation as a system responds to loss/changes and begins to explore alternative responses. The day emphasizes importance of differentiation of self for the transition leader and resources to help others understand current relationships. [11]

Bowen Family Systems Theory is not always utilized, but the language of systems theory is common among interims. Sometimes it may be applied as a weapon rather than a tool. Friedman noted that ". . . differentiation refers more to a process than a goal that can ever be achieved. When people say 'I differentiated from my wife, my child, my parent,' that proves they do not understand the concept."[12] The work of BFST in any context requires not only intellectual comprehension of concepts but also the willingness to have an emotional adventure in one's own family of origin.

Initially, the concepts of interim ministry were described as developmental tasks. In more recent work these are labeled as focus points. The change came about because all too often some interim ministers and denominational leaders discussed this as the work of experts and not of the congregation. In addition, the framework of tasks often became a checklist of activities to check off.

The Focus Points developed by the Interim Ministry Network may be thought of as areas for congregational attention. The Rev. John Keydel, an Episcopal priest and former President of the Interim Ministry Network presented a concise definition of the focus points in an essay in Transitional Ministry Today edited by Norman Bendroth. [13]

Each focus point is a place to ask questions and seek clarification from the congregation and its leaders about what pathway it has followed and where it says it wants to go in the future. These questions are ones that I have developed over time based on the work of Keydel, Bendroth and others such as Gil Rendle and Alice Mann.[14]

- Heritage: What are the stories that are told? What victories celebrated? What defeats acknowledged? Where has God been in time?
- Mission: Who are we presently? Where are we going? What has God called us to do in this time?
- Leadership: What are the gifts and skills that the membership holds? What gifts and skills are needed now? Who are the people in our midst who have them? How do we attain them if they are not present?
- Connections: Who is our neighbor? Who are our resource partners in church and community?

- Future: What is a faithful response to the ongoing mission and opportunity of this congregation?

In addition to the work of the congregation, David Sawyer identified five process tasks for an interim pastor. First, the pastor must enter the system and connect in meaningful ways. In short order the pastor must analyze what is happening in the congregation and decide how to proceed. The interim pastor must assume responsibility for decisions that need to be made. Finally, the pastor must leave when it is time.[15]

One congregation I served had an outdoor nativity. After the story of the birth of Jesus was enacted with all the attendant pageantry, Santa Claus appeared. The staff had some questions about the theological foundations of this depiction. But Santa was a beloved member of the church and it seems there not been much theological reflection about this presentation.

Based on staff input, I told "Santa" we would be going another way that year. He accepted it. Sometime later I was speaking with a young father in the hallway. The conversation was not about the pageant, but we ended up talking about it. He told me that "Someone decided that we couldn't have Santa this year!" He was upset about this. I responded: "I'm the one that decided that." This became the opportunity for a discussion which was useful as both of us had a chance to speak of the theological implications of who Santa was and what he represented.

It was also a chance for me to draw down on my own emotional work about claiming responsibility and credit (or blame) from family of origin work I had done for several years in the Leadership in Ministry workshops.

This was one of those occasions when a seeming happenstance conversation has deeper meaning and importance. Once he was aware that I took responsibility for the decision his demeanor changed. In addition, I am confident that the young father shared the substance of our conversation with others. Not only was I able to help him frame the situation theologically, but his comments helped me in my reflections.

A key to meaningful interim ministry is for the pastor in this time to assist the congregational leadership in identifying which focus area needs attention. Not all areas will command the same intensity or interest. The areas of exploration in an interim area are much like those when there is an installed pastor in place. However, the knowledge that this is an in between time and a sense of wanting to return to the normality of ordered ministry—to a sense of homeostasis—creates opportunities for meaningful service.

The role of Interim Pastor contains all aspects of the work of a pastoral leader, although they have a time bound relationship with the congregation. Interims provide a pastoral role; sermons will be preached and

Baptisms conducted. Communion will be served, pastoral visits made, meetings held, and plans made.

The ability of the pastor to function with less anxiety than others in the congregation or larger system will propel any progress that is made. As Edwin Friedman described it:

> . . .*members of the clergy function as transformers in an electric circuit. To the extent we are anxious ourselves, then, when anxiety in the congregation permeates our being, it becomes potentiated and feeds back into the congregational family at a higher voltage. But to the extent we can recognize and contain our own anxiety, then we function as step down transformers, or perhaps circuit breakers.* [16]

Anxiety is always present in a congregational system. The degree of that anxiety and its effect on the congregation's leaders, members and ministry is not the issue. What matters is how the anxiety is addressed. The way a pastoral leader engages anxiety will impact the outcome more than anything.

Adopting a framework of Bowen Family System Theory assists in addressing the tasks of the Interim, as well as in identifying how to approach the focus points of a congregation's life. Moreover, if a pastor has engaged in doing family of origin work, the theory becomes an invaluable resource for the task of leadership.

The work of becoming a "real" pastor is not defined by time as an ecclesiastical designation. Becoming a "real" pastor is the ability to function by being one's own self while finding ways for meaningful and useful connections to others.

NOTES:

[1]Norman Bendroth, *Interim Ministry in Action* (Rowman & Littlefield, 2018), pp. 1-8.

[2]Margery Williams, *The Velveteen Rabbit*. https://digital.library.upenn.edu/women/williams/rabbit/rabbit.html. Accessed May 4, 2020.

[3]Edwin H. Friedman, *A Failure of Nerve* (New York: Seabury Books, 2007), pp. 183-84.

[4]United Metodist Church Book of Discipline 2016. Secs 339-340, pp. 274-278. https://www.ctcumc.org/files/fileshare/2016-book-of-discipline.pdf. Accessed May 5, 2020; Presbyterian Church (U.S.A.). Book of Order, 2019-2021. G-2.0504, p. 34.

[5]Jonathan Edwards article in Wikipedia, https://en.wikipedia.org/wiki/Jonathan_Edwards_(theologian) Accessed May 5, 2020. Patricia J. Tracy, *Jonathan Edwards, pastor: Religion and society in eighteenth-century Northampton* (Wipf and Stock Publishers, 2006), pp. 171-194.

[6]New York Times, March 4, 1888.

[7]J.K. Rowling, *The Casual Vacancy* (New York: Little Brown and Company, 2012) p. 47.

[8]Loren Mead. *A Change of Pastors*, Alban, 2005, Pp. 82-85.

[9]Cited in Israel Galindo, *101 System Theory Quotes* (2016), p. 5.

[10]https://en.wikipedia.org/wiki/Johari_window. Accessed May 12, 2020.

[11]Interim Ministry Network Training, Day 1. Accessed May 6, 2020.

[12]Norman Bendroth, *Rethinking Interim Ministry,* posted April 6, 2012 at https://alban.org/archive/rethinking-transitional-ministry/. Accessed May 12, 2020; Friedman, pp. 183-84.

[13] (Rowan & Littlefield, 2015), pp. 53-62.

[14]Gil Rendle and Alice Mann. *Holy Conversations: Strategic Planning as a Spiritual Practice for Congregations* (Alban Institute, 2003).

[15]David Sawyer, "The Five Process Tasks of Transitional Ministry, " https://www.linkedin.com/pulse/five-process-tasks-transitional-ministry-david-sawyer , Accessed on May 13, 2020.

[16]Edwin H Friedman, *Generation to Generation* (New York: The Guilford Press, 1985) pp. 208-209

8

Reframing Helping Parents

Elaine Boomer

Parenting is hard! The world today is different from when I was a child or even when I was raising my own three children. There is more violence, more access to drugs, more information available to children and more pressure to ensure that our children become successful in life. And, as Roberta Gilbert says, "Parents are the hope for civilization." That's pressure!

Successful parenting is a concern for all parents and for those of us in the helping professions who counsel struggling parents. In today's environment, I see more and more parents engage in helicopter-parenting – parenting with an intense focus on how children function including school performance, sports performance, friends, dress, family involvement, speaking, etc. In other words, the child becomes the all-consuming focus of parents rather than self, marriage, and one's own functioning. Bowen

Family Systems offers a radically different framework to parenting.

Bowen Family Systems sheds light on what happens in families that impact parenting. Foremost is the concept of Nuclear Family Emotional Process as a foundation for what happens in family relationship dynamics. Secondly, there is the dynamic of how Triangles within the family system may impact children. A third concept is the Family Projection Process. These concepts, working together, help predict how children will be influenced in the family. How these phenomena work is generally out of our awareness but are neither good nor bad. Understanding the theory can help parents and counselors make changes that are in the best interest of the entire family.

In this article I will address three questions:

• What are the patterns or dynamics that affect how children function and grow into resilient adults?

• What must parents do to function as better parents?

• How can those in the helping professions assist families to function in ways that promote growth for the entire family?

Family Patterns and Dynamics

The nuclear family is an emotional unit. The child is a part of that unit – one piece of the larger whole. The result is that an action, an attitude, or emotion of one person in the family affects everyone else in the family. When a child has a problem, it is rarely an individual problem, rather, it points to an emotional or relationship issue in the family. Anxiety is the culprit for all of us. Anxiety is simply an increase in emotional turmoil arising from daily living – a job loss, a bad day, being tired, illness, a difficult boss, a fight with a friend – the list goes on and is a part of everyday living.

Anxiety is catching. It passes from one family member to another. Mom has a bad day at work and comes home to a messy house and Dad is watching TV. She criticizes Dad for not straightening up and starting dinner. Dad gets defensive or perhaps just shuts down. Now he has the anxiety. Five-year-old Tommy watches this and becomes whiney and difficult. Now Tommy has the anxiety. Tommy now pushes his brother, and the fight begins. Anxiety has spread throughout the family. Often this becomes a patterned triangle if the parents do not work out their differences and continue to focus on Tommy's behavior who may continue to act out. They come to perceive that Tommy is the one with the problem and begin to worry and focus on him.

In my family, I was often angry with my husband who was irresponsible with money. He alleviated his anger with me by focusing on our oldest daughter. She became his confidant, and she and I often butted heads. She began to act out, get poor grades, have poor relationships, and ultimately dropped out of school. Our focus was entirely on her. The problems between my husband and myself were never resolved. This was a patterned triangle that was years in the making and hampered this child's ability to function responsibly for many years.

Anxiety in a family with child-focus can manifest in many ways. A child can develop a mental illness, a physical condition, substance abuse, school truancy, or violence. Not every problem in a family stems from child-focus, but it certainly intensifies the situation. A child born with disabilities understandably sets the family up for child-focus but focus on the disabled child exclusively can exacerbate the issue and prevent the child from doing the best she can with her circumstances.

Certain children in the family get more focus than others. I worked with a family that had many children and was very chaotic and dysfunctional for generations. The last child in the family in two generations was the most functional of all the children. It is my assumption that the least amount of focus was on the youngest child enabling each of them to function better as adults. Extreme child focus and/or neglect have much to do with what is happening in the family. For example, a child coming after a still-birth or death of a child will tend to receive more focus. A divorce or parental death preceding a birth can result in more focus on the new child. Any number of circumstances in a family can increase anxiety and thus more focus on the child.

Functioning of Parents

Differentiation of Self. There are two important concepts that contribute to our children growing into high functioning adults. First is developing a strong sense of self, or, raising one's level of differentiation of self. A well differentiated parent knows what she thinks and is able to communicate by using "I" statements. In this case, principles drive functioning. This includes setting limits and boundaries that apply to everyone in the family.

Strong self-differentiation also means managing reactivity. Staying calm and using thinking rather than emotion to dictate behavior. Yelling and screaming gets us nowhere. In fact, it works in a perverse manner. Children cannot hear us when we are coming from a place of anger, frustration, and stress. It behooves us parents to take a breath, think, and then clearly state what we need to communicate. We can express our "feelings" calmly and allow natural consequences to determine outcome.

One of my daughters was skipping school. The school called hoping to get my help in preventing this. I was angry, of course, but managed to ask what the consequence was for skipping class. I was told that getting a zero was the result. It seemed natural to me that my daughter should receive the zero. Three zeroes constituted a failure in the class. I figured that if she failed that class, she would simply have to give up her summer for summer school. Talking to her about what I thought was the next step by simply stating the facts and giving her the choice.

A client of mine was frustrated and angry because her daughter wouldn't get up in the morning – was late every day and required a ride to school. After coaching, my client indicated that she would call her daughter once, and if she were late for school, she would have to call and pay for a taxi. No excuse note would be written. You can guess what happened next, the daughter was late again. She resisted calling the cab and argued, but mom held her ground. The second time it happened, the teenager automatically called the cab with no complaint. That was the end of that!

Allowing for the natural consequences of a child's poor behavior is always the best alternative. I encourage parents who are overly concerned about their child's grades/homework to simply set a time for study with no TV and devices and let the child take responsibility for his work. Parents can be available to assist but not hover. A natural consequence for poor school performance may be taking away privileges such as TV and device time or having to go to summer school.

Staying connected to our children is another component of differentiation of self. It is important to have "a personal relationship connection to each child in your family."[1] A personal relationship does not include emotionally charged negative messages, i.e. criticism, telling them what to think, sarcasm, ridicule, name-calling etc. These "negative messages make a lasting impression on the emotional brain often becoming a part of what people think about themselves for the rest of their life."[2] It requires calm open communication involving listening, asking questions and stating what you think.

Occasionally, even the best parents will have breakdowns or misunderstandings in communication with their children. This usually happens when we are tired, frustrated, or angry. Daniel Siegel, a renowned psychiatrist, calls this a "rupture." "Parents need to be able to understand their own behavior and emotions and how they may have contributed to the rupture in order to initiate a repair process."[3]

Breakdowns in communication without repair lead to deepening sense of disconnection between parent and child. Prolonged disconnection can create shame and humiliation that is toxic for the child's growing sense of self. Disconnections are a normal part of relationships. But parents must take responsibility for their actions. A repair in disconnection might go like this: "I am sorry I yelled at you when you came late for dinner. It was getting dark, and I was worried that something might have happened to you. I didn't mean to scare you by yelling so loudly, I went overboard and should have listened to you first and then told you what I was worried about."

It's really difficult to not impose your own agenda onto your child. Parental agendas may include promoting admirable values such as career choice, courage, thriftiness, kindness and discipline. This can vary from one child to another. When conflicts arise over agenda issues, over-vigilant parents see it as their responsibility to drive home their own points of view. For example: "You forgot your coat again. That's irresponsible and foolish" or "Because of your forgetfulness, you didn't feed the dog again and that's cruel." It is, however, important to share your values with your children. Consider how to communicate those sensitively. Listen empathetically first, addressing the child's feelings, then present some alternative behaviors. It involves more coaching than ordering or demanding. Labels aren't helpful. Understanding, asking questions, and setting boundaries facilitate this kind of communication.

Creating a Healthy Relationship With Your Spouse

The second most important concept in helping children become independent and high functioning is working on having a healthy relationship with your partner. When children are the intense focus in a family, there is a loss of focus on self by each parent. The parents' needs, interests and adult relationships take a second place to those of the child. Oddly, this can make the marriage/partnership of the parents seem to function better. Over time, however, parental relationships begin to flounder without time and attention. Anxiety will increase. Dysfunctional triangles will become more prevalent. This can lead to arguments, distance, and even divorce.

Because the family is an interlocking emotional-relationship system, all individuals in the family are affected by each other. Parents who don't address the difficulties in their relationship become victims to the anxiety that abounds. For example, mom is unhappy because her partner works too much, is distant and inattentive. Rather than address this, she focuses on one or more of the children, getting her much desired attention from them. Her partner feels more and more left out – works longer hours, maybe even has an affair. The emotional distance between the parents increases. Anxiety increases, and the child reacts by acting out, becoming shut down or developing physical or mental symptoms.

The child becomes the "problem" as the parents focus on the acting out behavior, rather than focusing on the parental relationship and its anxiety—the real cause of the matter. These patterns grind into ruts making it more and more difficult for the relationships to function cooperatively.

As Roberta Gilbert wrote, "As children see the grown-ups working on being more grown-up, they will predictably work on their own immaturities."[4]

Assisting Parents as Professionals

As a professional using a family systems framework, I find the most helpful approaches are listening and coaching by asking good questions. It is important that parents begin to understand that families are emotional systems – they develop interlocking patterns that affect every individual. I always draw a family genogram as they are talking to me. I'm looking for family dynamics and patterns, birth order, nodal events and generational patterns.

I find that two main facts are important in assessing what is happening in the family. One is the client's emotional process. Who is the distancer? Who is the pursuer? Who over-functions? Who under-functions? Who accommodates? Who is contrary? When a parent can identify their own patterns and work to make changes, the system begins to change. I'm also looking for triangles and ways to help the parents to better manage themselves in the triangle. One client had the habit of complaining about his wife to his mother. Although he felt better by joining with his mother, his wife felt demeaned and angry about it. I helped him see that he needed to address the problem with his wife, not his mother!

Secondly, I encourage parents to investigate their families of origin. Recognizing emotional patterns in the parents' families of origin is helpful in identifying repeating patterns in their nuclear family. I was amazed to discover that in the triangle with my oldest daughter, my husband and I were repeating a triangle from the two generations above me. Hidden agendas that parents unconsciously put onto their children often stem from the preceding generations. A parent that I worked with came from generations of doctors and lawyers. He pressured his son to do the same, but the son was very resistant. Was this due to the pressure working in a perverse manner, or did the son have other interests for his career?

Helping parents to reflect on their childhood experiences can help make sense of their own lives. A deeper self-understanding changes who you are. Making sense of your life enables you to understand others more fully and gives you the possibility of choosing your behaviors and expanding your repertoire of responses.

Coaching parents is slow but life-changing work. Everything takes a long time! Changing dysfunctional patterns and emotional processes produce profound changes.

Conclusion

When we become parents, we are given an incredible opportunity to grow as individuals and to create children who thrive in this complicated world. Unfortunately, parents can feel stuck in repetitive, unproductive patterns that don't support the loving, nurturing relationships that they envisioned when they began their roles as parents. Making sense of who they are, where they come from, and how they function can free parents from patterns of the past that imprison them in the present. Bowen Family Systems Theory offers some help in this regard. It is, in my opinion, the most life-changing and fruitful guidance that forever impacts our relationships with each member of the family and with others in our lives.

NOTES

[1]Roberta Gilbert. *Connecting with Our Children* (New York: John Wiley & Sons Inc. 2008), p. 139.
[2]Gilbert. *Connecting with Our Children*, p 145.

[3]Daniel Siegel. *Parenting from the Inside Out* (New York: Penquin Putnam Inc., 2003), p. 145.

[4]Gilbert. *Connecting with Our Children,* p. 114.

9

Reframing Preaching

Meg Hess

The possible starting points for reframing preaching through a lens of Bowen Family Systems Theory are multiple. In this chapter, my focus is to use BFST as a hermeneutic, a theory and method of interpretation, for how we think about preaching in a community of faith. I use some of the concepts of BFST such as Anxiety, Togetherness and Individuality instincts, Family Emotional Process, Differentiation of Self, and Triangles to explore aspects of the function of preaching to the emotional system of the congregation. I hope these musings invite your own thinking about how a systems approach can enrich the preaching life.

Preacher Formation: Relational Acoustics, Politics of Talk and Family of Origin

My call to preaching came to me in a dream. I was in the pulpit of the First Baptist Church of Danville,

Virginia, where I grew up. I was expected to preach, but had no sermon, no scripture passage, nothing. The full congregation looked at me with what I experienced as skeptical judgment. I was terrified. Then I noticed a man sitting on the front row. He was leaning forward with a look of hopeful expectation on his face. It was as if he was saying: "Go ahead Meg, you have something to say." The man was Dr. L.D. Johnson, former pastor of that church. He had dedicated me as a baby.

At the very least, I felt the dream was a blessing. In a church that had never ordained women and only recently had begun to invite women to be Deacons, someone was listening to me; at least in my dreams.

In their work *Meeting at the Crossroads: Women's Psychology and Girls' Development*, Brown and Gilligan trace the impact of relationship on voice as they explore "relational acoustics."

> Voice is inherently relational—one does not require a mirror to hear oneself—yet. The sounds of one's voice change in resonance depending on the relational acoustics: whether one is heard or not heard, how one is responded to (by oneself and by other people.[1]

In my years of teaching preaching at Andover Newton Theological Seminary as an Adjunct Professor, I witnessed men and women sort through what it meant to find their voice for preaching. New preachers were supported or silenced by the relational acoustics of both congregation and society. Yet it was most often in their family of origin that my students first learned rules around speech and silence. The impact of being heard or not heard in that early context as they sought to differentiate a Self frequently showed up in preaching class. Those who were "heard into speech," to use feminist theologian Nelle Morton's phrase, were supported in growing a Self.[2] They at least had a muscle memory of using their voice as a starting place of their formation as a preacher. Others had more work to do to discover and express their voice in preaching.

In preaching courses, I invited students to tease out the threads of the relational acoustics in their family of origin as they explored the beginnings of their preaching voice. In *Women's Ways of Knowing: The Development of Self, Voice, and Mind*, Mary Field Belenky and others used the phrase "the politics of talk" to explore one's development of voice in the family context. "By this (politics of talk) we mean those forms of discourse that a family permits and encourages and those that they minimize and prohibit."[3]

Here are questions I used with students to help them think about the impact of their family of origin on their formation as preachers:

- How would you describe "the politics of talk" in your family of origin?
- Was curiosity welcomed in your family of origin?

- Did questions in your family draw out and explore feelings, ideas, plans, and the possibilities for compromises? Or did the questions silence and constrict?
- Were people invited to figure out what they thought? If you disagreed, were you considered "stupid" or was your opinion explored to be better understood?
- How much pressure was there to go along with "group think," how much freedom was given to differ?
- Did you generally feel heard or not heard in your family of origin?
- How might these family of origin dynamics be influencing your preaching today?

A preacher who gains clarity about the impact of their family of origin's relational acoustics and politics of talk can explore whether any unresolved family of origin issues are presently impacting their preaching. One of the places where those issues may show up is in the preacher's experience of, and response to, anxiety in the system.

Anxiety and Preaching

The fear of public speaking, *glossophobia,* is not limited to preachers. I've heard it claimed that many people fear public speaking more than death. BFST invites preachers to consider that their own anxiety around preaching may be more than a pedestrian fear of public speaking. What may seem like an individual experience of anxiety may be a manifestation of our relationship to a system's anxious emotional process.

Anxiety is a response to a threat. The brain cannot always distinguish between a real or imagined threat. As mentioned elsewhere, some of the familiar responses to anxiety are fight, flight, freeze, flock, fawn, and fix. Part of the formation of the preacher involves becoming a student of one's own anxiety. This involves noticing when anxiety is triggered, how it manifests in one's body and one's thinking, and coming up with strategies to calm self while claiming one's voice for preaching. It also invites the preacher to consider that anxiety can also be a collective experience, passed around an emotional system through relational dynamics.

Preachers may experience anxiety around preaching for a variety of reasons. One may be that in finding and using their voice, they are challenging the "politics of talk" or "relational acoustics" of their family of origin. Or stating a view or principle that separates them from the togetherness force dominant in the congregation that could activate an anxious response, in the preacher as well as listener.

The sibling position of the preacher in the family of origin may also impact how anxiety shows up in their preaching experience. An oldest may be used to being listened to in a way that may or may not be replicated in the preaching relationship. Or, anxiety might be constellated in a youngest who always feels like everyone else knows way more than they do and assumes they will not be listened to or taken seriously. Identifying how these dynamics affect a preacher's ability to differentiate a self in preaching is an important aspect of claiming one's voice for preaching or in moving beyond crippling anxiety around preaching.

A preacher's role in their family of origin around anxiety can also show up in their preaching. Everyone in a family has some role around anxiety in that system. There is the igniter or generator of anxiety, the amplifier of anxiety, the absorber of anxiety, the dampener of anxiety, and the leader who can calm the system's anxiety with thoughtful responses to acute or chronic anxiety. The preacher may unconsciously occupy one of the functions around anxiety, fanning the flames of anxiety in a way that does not serve the system or inventing anxiety where it does not exist. The preacher may also absorb the anxiety through illness. The effective preacher is aware of where anxiety is showing up in the system and can thoughtfully take that into account when constructing and delivering sermons.

Preaching and the Differentiation of Self Scale

The presence of chronic and acute anxiety in the congregational system invites the congregational leader to thoughtfully consider how they differentiate a Self as a preacher. The BFST concept of Differentiation of Self has internal and external dimensions. It acknowledges the tension between the two life instincts of togetherness and individuality. "On the intrapsychic level, differentiation of self is the capacity to balance emotional and logical processes; on the interpersonal level, it is the ability to create intimate, emotional ties with others whilst remaining on some level independent from them."[4]

Bowen developed a Differentiation of Self Scale as an effort to note the differences between those with higher or lower levels of Differentiation. Though Bowen used numbers between 0 and 100 for the scale, it is not an assessment tool but rather a metaphor whose function is "…a way of calling attention to the fact of variation in human emotional functioning and a Basis for it."[5] I am using the theoretical construct of the scale to think about the functioning of preachers.

At the Lower End of the Scale

People functioning at the lower end of the scale have a less Differentiated Self. They "…depend so heavily on the acceptance and approval of others that they either quickly adjust what they think, say, and do to please others or they dogmatically proclaim what others should be like and pressure them to conform."[6]

The following list reflects my thinking about how the lower level of Differentiation of Self shows up in the preacher and their preaching.

- Is restricted by "politics of talk" from one's family of origin
- Reactive self-censoring results in not being able to share one's true thinking
- Sense of worth or value as a preacher primarily is tied to external praise or criticism
- Selection of sermon text/topic/theme is driven by "the crisis of the week"
- No working definition or theology of preaching. Doesn't have a clear sense of the focus, aim, or purpose of a sermon, resulting in a disorganized, chaotic, or difficult to follow sermon
- Unwilling to try new styles or approaches to preaching: fixed, rigid, or formulaic approach. Assumes there is a "right" way to interpret text determined by experts
- Preaching is reactive, driven by anxiety or un-examined opinions

- The preacher is overwhelmed by or unaware of anxiety in the system and of the congregation's emotional process
- Is unaware of the dynamics of the preaching triangle. Gets caught in the burn out position of the emotional triangles and feels fully responsible for how the congregation responds to the sermon
- Preaching is characterized by a willfulness or determination to convince or change the listener. Overly attached to the outcome of getting the listeners to buy into the sermon's point of view
- Draws heavily upon external sources for sermon development—commentaries, on-line sermons, canned pulpit resources—rather than develop one's thinking
- Inability to regulate the flooding of physical anxiety symptoms which prohibits self-regulation and a grounded connection with body in the pulpit.

At the Upper End of the Scale

A person who functions higher up the Differentiation of Self Scale can take defining stands, self-regulate in the face of resistance or push-back behavior, while staying emotionally connected to everyone in the system. According to Bowen Theory,

A person with a well-differentiated "self" recognizes his realistic dependence on others, but he can stay calm and clear headed enough in the face of conflict, criticism, and rejection to distinguish thinking rooted in a careful assessment of the facts from thinking clouded by emotionality. Thoughtfully acquired principles help guide decision-making about important family and social issues, making her less at the mercy of the feelings of the moment. What she decides and what she says match what she does.[7]

For a preacher, differentiation assumes the ability to be congruent with who they are both in and out of the pulpit. The description on the Georgetown Family Center site describes one functioning higher up the Scale as "Confident in his thinking, he can support other's views without being a disciple or reject others' views without polarizing the differences. He defines himself without being pushy and deals with pressure to yield without being wishy-washy."[8]

Here is my thinking about the characteristics of a preacher who functions higher on the Differentiation of Self Scale:

- Has differentiated from the "politics of talk" in one's family of origin enough to state one's opinion, take a stand, and find one's voice in an emotional system

- Thinks through appropriate timing of speaking one's mind and allows space for response, reactions, or resistance to sermon
- Selection of sermon text, topic, and theme is guided by an overall plan, with flexibility to respond to issues or events that come up
- Has a good working definition of effective preaching and can self-evaluate one's sermons
- Is committed to one's growth as a preacher Experiments with new types of sermons, reflects on their effectiveness, and incorporates new insights into preaching
- Knows how anxiety affects oneself when preaching, has found ways to regulate self, be rooted in an embodied preaching
- Engages creatively with the text, integrates one's own experience of the text with information from commentaries and other sources.
- Preaching is pro-active, or responsive, thoughtfully considering one's principles, beliefs, and theological stance
- Maintains a neutral position in the preaching triangle. Leaves the outcome of the sermon between God and the congregation or between text and congregation
- Preaching is characterized by a strong sense of Self in relationships. The preacher is open to being

changed by the preaching process and invites
listeners to join them in that transformation process

- The preacher is aware of the anxiety and emotional
process of the congregational system. Uses the
function of preaching to "preach to the system."

These are descriptors of a range of functioning in
the formation of the preacher. Rather than hearing them as
a judgment, my hope is that these ideas invite preachers to
move toward a more thoughtful, less anxious engagement
with preaching.

Triangles and Preaching

Preachers and listeners have opinions about what
makes a sermon effective. Most preachers have
experienced parishioners coming up to them after a
sermon and expressing wildly different versions of what
they heard. The BFST concept of the emotional triangle
offers a way of thinking about the dynamics between the
preacher, the listener, and the sermon.

The Third Room of Preaching

Marianne Gaarden, a Bishop in the Lutheran-
Evangelical Church of Denmark, conducted an empirical
study of how congregants listen to sermons. Her
conclusions offer a way of thinking about the Preaching

Triangle and to reframe preaching as a relational, dynamic act of meaning-making. When Gaarden asked listeners about a sermon, their initial response was to say whether they liked or disliked the preacher.

The more the preacher was experienced as authentic, the more the listener felt invited to engage in the creation of meaning as they listened. To put it another way: when a preacher brings her authentic, congruent self rather than her false or pseudo-self into the preaching event it strengthens the connection on the side of the triangle between preacher and listener.

Gaarden used the metaphor of "the third room of preaching" to describe preaching as a collaborative co-construction of the sermon. It is in this "polyphonic room" where the sermon is formed between speaker and listener. The true self of the preacher invites the listener to a true, emotional, and thoughtful responses to the preaching event.

This polyphony creates a room, where the churchgoers, through different kinds of dialogical interaction, categorized as associative, critical, and contemplative, create new meaning and understanding. It is not a room that the listener or the preacher can control or occupy, but a room that both engage in.[9]

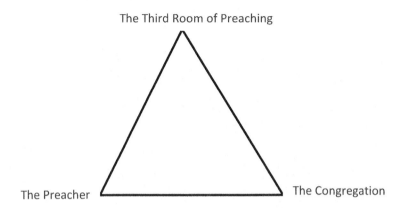

The Third Room of Preaching

The Preacher

The Congregation

The concept of "the third room of preaching" invites the preacher to define Self in the preaching triangle by clarifying the thoughts, beliefs, principles, and theology in their sermons. It also affirms the importance of the preacher's maintaining relational connection with the congregation. The Third Room allows the preacher to hold the outcome of the sermon more lightly as the listener co-constructs the sermon. The preacher is responsible for thoughtfully constructing and delivering their sermon, but what the listener ultimately does with the sermon is not their responsibility.

Dealing with Criticism in the Preaching Triangle

One place where the dynamics of the Preaching Triangle emerges is around dealing with criticism. I've coached many preachers on how to shift their response to criticism of their preaching. Preachers often share that when someone criticizes their preaching, that they immediately became defensive, upset, or angry. Their go-to responses range from arguing about the content to trying to convert the critic to their point of view to dismissing the criticism and distancing themselves from the critic. Or, they completely buy into the criticism and decide that they should never preach again. Wrong or right thinking about criticism (the critic is totally right or completely wrong) does not allow for a nuanced assessment of the criticism. Using BFST as a framework to think about this issue gives preachers other options.

For example, when invited to consider Edwin Friedman's notion that "criticism is a form of pursuit," preachers can expand their perspective. Getting curious about why a critic is moving toward them through criticism helps preachers turn down the volume on the content of the critique. This helps to take the criticism less personally as they observe the relational dynamics of closeness and distance. The preacher can take a deep breath, down regulate, and think: "This person is moving toward me. I could respond with fight (arguing) or flight (distancing). Or maybe there's another option." Having some go-to responses such as "Thank you for sharing what you heard in the sermon" or "I'd like to hear more about your thinking on this issue" or even "What is it like for you when I say something from the pulpit that you disagree with" is a way to connect with someone who is moving toward you. Essentially, the preacher is considering how to be more neutral in the triangle around criticism. Taking criticism of one's preaching less personally also makes space for thoughtfully exploring the critique, mining it for possible value, and discarding what isn't useful.

A Differentiated Preacher as key to the Function of Preaching

I sat through hundreds of sermons as a child: coloring on the cover of the Sunday bulletin, swinging my feet, digging into my father's coat pocket for a mint, wondering when the sermon would ever end. Had you asked me then "what is the purpose of preaching?" I would have said it was to bore small children to death. As I grew older, I noticed a pattern: always the sermon was followed by an altar call. The organ played and people walked down the aisle to commit their lives to Christ while the congregation sang "Just as I Am" one more time. The purpose of preaching was to save the lost, to motivate and propel the sinners and the backsliders down that aisle through guilt or fear of eternal damnation. Being an impressionable and anxious child, I took that walk more than once.

As a student in preaching class in seminary, I heard classic descriptions of preaching's purpose that echoed my early experience of the willfulness of preaching. Preaching was to convince, to exhort, to persuade, or to motivate the listener to act or change or believe in a certain way.

Oversimplifications certainly, these approaches held the assumption that preaching was about getting others to change. I bought into that understanding of the function for a long time, but my thinking, and framework, about the function(s) of preaching has shifted.

The late 19th century preacher Phillips Brooks defined preaching as "communication of truth through personality." His definition invites a reframing of preaching from willing others to belief and action, to bringing one's full Self to the preaching task. The function of preaching will vary according to where the congregation is in their life cycle and how and when the emotional process of a congregation is addressed in a sermon. Ultimately, the job of the preacher is to identify openings where they may address the deeper emotional process dynamics of a congregation in a way that invites change, growth, healing, connection, and maturation. Ideally, we can engage with freedom in our ongoing preacher formation of Differentiating a Self. God invites us, as God invited Ezekiel, "to preach, whether they hear or do not hear." (Ezekiel 3:11).

NOTES:

[1]Lyn Mikel Brown, and Carol Gilligan, *Meeting at the Crossroads: Women's Psychology and Girl's Development* (Cambridge, MA: Harvard University Press, 1992), p. 20.

[2]Nelle Morton, *The Journey Is Home* (Boston: Beacon Press, 1985).

[3]Mary Field Belenky et al. 1986. *Women's Ways of Knowing: The Development of Self, Voice, and Mind* (New York: Basic Books, Inc., 1986), p. 156.

[4]Michael E. Kerr & Murray Bowen, *Family Evaluation* (New York: W.W. Norton & Co, 1988); Murray Bowen, *Family Therapy in Clinical Practice* (New York: Jason Aronson, 1978).

[5]Michael Kerr, *Bowen Theory's Secrets: Revealing the Hidden Life of Families* (New York: W.W. Norton and Company, 2019), p. 60.

[6]See the Georgetown Family Center website www.thebowencenter.org/ differentiation-of-self

[7]Ibid.

[8]Ibid.

[9]Marianne Gaarden, *The Third Room of Preaching: The Sermon, The Listener, and the Creation of Meaning* (Westminster John Knox Press, 2017).

10

Reframing Pastor and Staff Reviews

Keith Harder

P astoral reviews of one kind or another are endemic in congregations. I have personally been through three pastoral reviews and assisted with more than a dozen reviews of other pastors, all in Mennonite settings. Mennonite congregations have a lot of latitude on whether regular reviews happen, when they happen or how much the congregation's judicatory is involved. Some Mennonite conferences are trying to regularize reviews. To that end I am part of a team that is available to congregations to assist with reviews.

There are informal and formal reviews. Every interaction with a parishioner, every committee and board meeting, every event, every public appearance, every vote or decision about tenure provides the occasion for feedback, a kind of informal review. The question is: Am I paying attention to the feedback? Am I learning what there is to be learned from the feedback I am receiving? Am I using these occasions as opportunities to grow in self-awareness and self-differentiation?

I find myself asking what a formal pastoral review would look like if done from a BFST framework. Most reviews I have been involved with tend to focus on performance (e.g., preaching, administration, pastoral care) which has to do with meeting congregant's explicit expectations of what they want from their pastor. They tend to focus on the pastor's job description which describes the pastor's role and explicit expectations. Is the pastor doing what we hired her to do? Are congregants satisfied with what the pastor is doing?

I was recently reminded that there may be more to what is expected of pastors than their formal or explicit role or job description. There may also be implicit expectations; the impact we expect her to have on the congregation, e.g., be the catalyst of numerical growth, keep everything on an even keel, keep everyone happy, generate new programs but don't rock the boat too much, challenge us, but not too much.

Whether they be explicit or implicit, trying to meet parishioner expectations represents a fundamental tension. That is, how does my sense of self and purpose, my self differentiation, mesh or conflict with what others expect of me and how will I navigate this tension?

BFST also tells us that these role expectations and functions happen in an emotional field that affects how people experience and evaluate them. Having some awareness of the emotional field, or what is sometimes called "reading the room,"and navigating in that field will go a long way in determining how fruitful pastors will be. Can they accurately recognize the elements of this emotional field? Is the emotional field of the congregation relatively calm or anxious, stable or conflicted, open to new ideas or stuck with the way it has always been?

Can they navigate within it as a "non-anxious presence," and with "non-reactive persistence,"as Edwin Friedman phrases, or as a differentiated self?

What if we framed our reviews with this emotional field or context in view? What if we gave more attention to how pastors navigate in this emotional minefield?

In my experience a pastoral review can itself be a source of anxiety for the person being reviewed, those in the congregation charged with conducting the reviews, judicatory leaders, even the pastor's family. After one review, I was struck by how my children were affected. In some ways they felt that our whole family was being evaluated.

How might we address whatever anxiety the pastor brings to a review? One answer might be to engage the pastor as much as possible in the review and address any sense that he may think he is a victim of the review process; that it is happening *to* him. To this end I have long believed that pastoral reviews should begin with a self-evaluation. This could include questions about his or her job description and other more implicit functions. It could also involve questions about how the pastor is "reading the room," interprets the emotional field of the congregation, and how he or she is interacting with it.

For example, we could ask the pastor to "Recall and reflect on a time when you were in conflict with someone in the congregation." Or more specifically, "Recall and reflect on a time when you had a significant difference or conflict with a lay leader in the congregation."

The written response could be a descriptive narrative, and/or it could include asking the pastor to choose from a variety of adjectives such as: I was... thoughtful, inquisitive, reactive, judgmental, patient, impatient, creative, ill at ease, relaxed, nervous, secure, defensive.

Another example could be to invite the pastor to think about a time when she became aware of an unmet need. Did I overfunction, underfunction, delegate responsibility to meet the need, take on the responsibility to meet the need myself, avoid thinking about the need hoping someone would take care of the situation?

Or we could ask: How do I maintain my purpose and sense of self in the face of pressure to give in to expectations that conflict with my calling and purpose?

The pastor's reflection on these questions could provide a window into the level of self-differentiation of the pastor. At the very least this mode of inquiry could help the pastor think about the emotional field in the congregation and how she operates in it. It might be a lens through which the pastor could even grow in her self-awareness.

These questions are based on the first and second basic tenants of BFST:

1. We always operate in an emotional system
2. How we operate in that system will reflect our degree of self differentiation; our capacity to think about our situation and functioning before reflexively reacting to it.

In addition, these questions invite reflection on the level of anxiety in the pastor and the congregational system. Bowen theory posits that the more anxious the system, the more it will challenge and reveal our degree of differentiation.

What other elements of BFST could inform and enhance pastoral reviews? We could ask how triangles are in play. When people are anxious with another person, or anxious about an issue or decision, they tend to involve a third person to help manage their anxiety. We could ask whether the pastor is able to recognize triangles and stay differentiated within them. Is the pastor absorbing anxiety in the system when people seek to triangle him in managing their anxiety? Can the pastor resist the anxiety of the review being projected onto him and possibly becoming the identified patient in the system?

Are there indicators of people distancing from each other or the congregation as a way of dealing with differences or conflict or the review itself? Is the pastor seeking to project his anxiety onto others by triangleing with others or absorbing anxiety from others? Are there indicators of cut offs in the congregation or in the functioning of the pastor?

What are the inter-generational dynamics at play in the congregation or in the pastor's own life? What is the influence of the congregation's founders? Of dominant and influential families? Of trauma or great achievement in the history of the congregation? I recently heard of a long-time member of a congregation say that his congregation has always been hard on its pastors, reminiscent of Edwin Friedman's comment that there are congregations that are pills or plums. How are any of these dynamics of the past playing out in the present?

How is the pastor's sibling position in her family of origin playing out? Are there people in the congregation, especially its leadership, that trigger reactions in the pastor that may resemble dynamics the pastor grew up with? For example, is someone in lay leadership functioning like an older brother who over-functioned in the pastor's family of origin.

How is the emotional field in the community where the congregation is located affecting the emotional field within the congregation? What is the place of the congregation in the community? How is the economy in the community where the congregation is located? What is the racial, cultural composition of the community? Are traumatic events in the community impacting the congregation?

These are some questions based on the tenets of BFST that may provide avenues of inquiry into the emotional field of the congregation and/or the functioning of a pastor. Not all of these variables will be equally in play in a given congregation or a pastor's situation but all could be. Asking questions along these lines could help identify key factors that are affecting a given pastor's situation in any given congregation?

For example, as part of a general survey, congregants could be asked to circle terms that they think apply to their congregation from a range of options such as: anxious, relaxed, conflicted, fearful, confident, secure, unsettled, hopeful, lively, lifeless.

Congregants could also be asked to circle terms that they think apply to their pastor with a focus on how the pastor navigates the emotional process in the congregation. Our pastor is: thoughtful, has a good sense of humor, defensive, approachable, secure, anxious, creative, intense, relaxed, controlling.

How else might we assess which factors are in play or most salient in the life and ministry of pastors and congregation?

Apart from asking questions about the emotional field in the congregation or the pastor's functioning in a written questionnaire, these kinds of questions could be included in interviews of congregational leaders or in focus groups. Asking questions suggests that the answers are in the congregation, not in the expertise of an outside expert.

Thinking about this topic I find myself wondering how best to make use of BFST when people may not know anything about the theory or its jargon. What terminology reflects and communicates the insight of the theory without falling back on theory jargon. Earlier I suggested "reading the room" or "implicit expectations" as ways to talk about emotional field, or emotional maturity or emotional intelligence as other ways to talk about self-differentiation. How do we communicate the insights about triangles or cut off or inter-generational emotional transmission? Maybe we simply need to make the effort to explain these elements of BFST when they seem to be in play.

This paper only offers reflections on the overall perspective with which we approach pastoral reviews. The work of translating this perspective into evaluation tools and formats (interview questions, questionnaires, focus group formats) remains. Hopefully this overview Bowen theory might help in the development of those tools and clarify what we are looking for and what we see in whatever tools we use.

So, as I close these reflections I wonder again, what is the purpose of pastoral reviews? What are we looking for? What signals to us that a pastor is successful or competent or faithful to her calling? Are these even the right measures?

In preparing for this presentation, I remembered a paper by Larry Matthews called "Leadership Viewed Through a Family Systems Lens" that was written in 2002. In that paper, Larry outlined three aspects of self-differentiation. The first is self-regulation, "the task of regulating one's anxiety, the internal dimension of growing in self-differentiation." The second is "self-definition," which he calls the external dimension, "the task of communicating self to other selves." "To define self is to give expression to the thoughts, values and goals one holds dear." He calls this "one of my major tasks as a pastor. My responsibility is to get clear about what I think and believe and communicate those thoughts and beliefs in words and actions, not to get others straight about what they should think and believe."

He goes on to say that "self-differentiating leaders work at self-regulation and self-regulation while maintaining connection to their relational systems." He says that "Friedman referred to a leader's ability to maintain a posture of non-reactive persistence—staying connected and on course in the face of resistance – as the "key to the kingdom."

In a concluding word of caution Larry writes, "This understanding of leadership focuses upon the leader and not upon the outcome of the leader's efforts. Viewed through the emotional process lens of family systems theory, leadership is not about them or success but about self – self-regulation, self-definition, self-differentiation. The payoff is self."

These words of wisdom speak to the purpose of pastoral reviews. If focusing on outcomes and meeting the expectations of others is fool's gold, the gold standard according to Bowen Family Systems Theory is:

Self-regulation, remaining calm
Self-definition, remaining clear
And staying connected.

11

Reframing the Ethics of Helping

Margaret Marcuson

One of the most significant developments in my own thinking over the last several years has been my exposure to Bowen Family Systems Theory, developed by Murray Bowen, particularly as expressed in the work of Edwin H. Friedman, author of *Generation to Generation: Family Process in Church and Synagogue*. I also studied with him in his Postgraduate Seminars in Family Emotional Process. His ideas have revolutionized my thinking, my ministry and my life — I say this without exaggeration! The theory has given me a new framework for life and ministry.

A key part of Bowen theory is the concept of "differentiation of self." Friedman defined differentation in this way: "the capacity...to define his or her own life goals and values apart from surrounding togetherness pressures, to say 'I' when others are demanding 'you' and 'we.' It includes the capacity to maintain a (relatively) non-anxious presence in the midst of anxious systems, to take maximum responsibility for one's own destiny and emotional being....Differentiation means the capacity to be an 'I' while remaining connected."[1]

Differentiation is different from individuation or autonomy in that it means both being a self and remaining connected to others. Can we be clear about who we are and about our deepest values while remaining connected emotionally to our parents, our spouses, our troublesome church members, our denomination?

Murray Bowen hypothesized a scale of differentiation, from the least mature to the most mature, and suggested that all human beings fall on this continuum, with no one higher than about 70 (out of 100). Where we fall on this scale depends largely on where our parents and previous generations were, and what our place in our own family is. Siblings may be higher or lower on the scale depending on various factors in the family (birth order, sibling position, family stress at the time of birth, other family history factors). We tend to marry individuals with similar ranges.

Those who are less well-differentiated have less well-developed individuality. Their togetherness needs are very strong. Michael Kerr describes the very poorly differentiated person this way: "[His] individuality is practically non-existent. His emotional reactions are easily triggered, intense and prolonged, and he has almost no psychological development that permits him to be a separate person… As differentiation increases, individuality is better developed, togetherness needs are less intense, and emotional reactiveness is better modulated."[3]

Those who are better differentiated (have more "self") may or may not have fewer apparent social, psychological and physical symptoms and problems than others. But they are better equipped to deal with the crises of life, have greater resiliency and recuperative powers, are less stressed.[4] The focus is on the response rather than the condition. Friedman wrote, that given the same objective circumstances, families or individuals are more likely to dysfunction or develop symptoms to the extent that their differentiation is low, and to tolerate more symptoms or rebound better from intense crises to the extent that their differentiation is high.

Friedman expressed his view of the scale of differentiation as a "focus on strength rather than pathology. It comes up fully on the side of personal responsibility rather than faulting the stars, society, the environment, or one's parents, for that matter. . . differentiation is inherently an antivictim, antiblaming focus…precisely because differentiation is a focus on the individual's response, it refuses to allow the system to take all the responsibility"[6]

Can people increase their level of differentation and thereby improve their response to their environment? Yes, if they are willing to work on defining a self while still remaining connected to important people in their lives. They have to be willing to face the emotional reactivity which will occur.

Another Bowen concept is that of homeostasis (balance). A system, including a family system, achieves a certain balance over time. There is an interdependency among the parts. When one part (e.g., a family member) makes a change, it upsets the balance. The other parts will try to restore the balance. If one person begins to act in a more mature manner, the others may act more immature in order to bring things back into balance. To truly develop greater differentiation, one must stay on course in the face of reactions which amount to attempted sabotage of the effort toward differentiation.[6]

For example, a wife who has submerged herself in her marriage and children may decide she needs to develop more of a self. She may decide to go back to school. One of her children may develop serious problems at school, or her husband may begin drinking. Her task in increasing differentiation is not to adapt to the symptom, which might mean dropping out of school, but to calmly continue with her own path while staying emotionally connected to her family. This illustration shows just how challenging the path of increasing differentiation can be.

Another concept in Bowen theory is the notion of the emotional field, or emotional system. This refers to any group of people (or other form of life, for that matter) which has become interdependent, has some level of organization and intercommunication. The structure, or field, comes to influence the parts more than the parts influence the functioning of the system. This is true of ant colonies, human bodies, families and churches.

Friedman suggested, "A family emotional system includes the members' thoughts, feelings, emotions, fantasies, associations and past connections, individually and together. It includes their physical makeup, genetic heritage, and current metabolic states. It involves their sibling position and their parents' sibling positions. It rotates on the axes of their respective paths within the multigenerational processes transmitted from their own families of origin, including the fusion and the cutoffs. It includes the emotional history of the system itself, particularly the conditions under which it originally took shape..."[7] In other words, a family emotional system is big!

The term "emotional field," sometimes used instead of "emotional system," is useful because of the analogy with fields in nature. No one has ever seen a magnetic field, or a gravitational field, just as we cannot see emotional fields. These fields are inferred from the predictable ways metals, or planets, or people, behave in their presence.[8]

The emotional field in a given family results in members coming to occupy differing functioning positions within the family. For example, most people are aware of the different characteristics generally associated with different sibling positions within the family. Oldest children tend to feel and act responsible for younger children, whether or not parents encourage this behavior.[9]

Functioning positions operate in reciprocal relationship to one another. Someone who "overfunctions," takes greater responsibility in the relationship or in the system, relates to another who "underfunctions," takes less responsibility. They each shape the attitudes, feelings and behavior of the other. The overfunctioning person feels responsible for the emotional well-being of the other, and works (often very hard) to make up for perceived deficiency in the other's functioning. The under-functioning person is dependent on the other.[10] Our tennis-playing couple clearly illustrate this pattern.

Relationships within the emotional field can differ depending on the level of differentiation. The greater the level of differentiation, the greater the flexibility of the relationship. People at lower levels of differentiation, at lower maturity, depend more on important relationships for their functioning and sense of well-being. People at higher levels of differentiation can move closer or farther away from one another without being threatened. They are not dependent on each other's acceptance and approval for their sense of self. At lower levels of differentiation, people have a less well developed sense of self, and are more dependent upon the relationship.[11] They are more likely to adapt to one another in order to preserve the relationship, or, conversely, exhibit extreme emotional reactivity within the relationship. In the classic church fight about carpet color, both the person who wants to keep the peace at all costs and the person who furiously insists on green or red demonstrate low levels of differentiation.

The presence of what is known as chronic anxiety affects all of relationships, and all of life itself. Chronic anxiety is not what we think of as being overtly "anxious" about something. It is the emotional and physical reactivity of all protoplasm. It is a quality humans share with all of life. For people, "the principal generators of chronic anxiety are reactions to a disturbance in the balance of a relationship system."[12] So, an event such as a birth or a death in a family can disturb the family system, but anxiety that is chronic comes more from how people deal with the disturbance: their reaction to the disturbance of the emotional field rather than their reaction to the event itself. A significant death where reaction is extreme can disturb the balance of a family for generations.[13]

According to Bowen theory, chronic anxiety is the root cause of all symptoms, whether physical, emotional or relational.[14] Friedman suggested that the antidote to the presence of chronic anxiety, and the preventive medicine, always is differentiation.

As a pastor I have always felt that my goal was to promote growth. Friedman offers a model of leadership through self-differentiation. The implications of this for me are that if I mature, as I mature, there is a corresponding jump up in the level of maturity of any group I lead. Of course, this does not occur without some reaction, some attempted sabotage. The principle of homeostasis tells us that any system will work to restore the status quo. But a concerted effort even in the face of reactivity can change the nature of a system.

In 1970 the results of some research were published in which individual organisms from a species that had not evolved immune systems were moved toward one another in increasingly greater degree of proximity. What was observed was that at a certain distance the smaller organism began to disintegrate, and within twenty-four hours had lost the principles of its organization completely. The larger organism did nothing to attack the smaller. The smaller organism disintegrated as a result of its own metabolic processes functioning in relation to the proximity of the other.[15]

According to Friedman, these findings "suggest that the major problem of families may not be to get members to be closer, but to enable them to be clearer about where they end and others in their life begin. Most of the helping professions seem to be largely concerned with promoting proximity rather than differentiation, despite the fact that the natural movement of protoplasm seems to be toward other protoplasm. In other words, the basic problem in families may not be to maintain relationships, rather, to maintain the self that permits nondisintegrative relationships."[16]

These concepts: differentiation, emotional fields or systems, homeostasis and chronic anxiety provide a beginning framework for understanding Bowen theory. So what does all this have to do with theology? Friedman did some informal theological reflection which may serve as a beginning point.

Friedman viewed the very nature of evil as invasive and unregulated. He noted that all pathogens, whether they are viruses, malignant cells or troublesome people, lack self-regulation. All things that lack self-regulation are both invasive of neighbor space and cannot learn from their experience.[17]

Individuals who are the troublemakers in a family or an institution are always invasive of their neighbor's space. Predator organizations, whether totalitarian nations or organized crime, operate like a virus or a cancer cell.[18] Friedman suggested that almost all immoral or unethical activity can be understood as a disorder of the self. The unethical or immoral person is aggrandizing the self, making themselves more important than they really are.[19]

Friedman put the whole issue this way, "All immoral behavior, meaning relational initiatives that are manipulative of others, may be understood as a form of dependency. The unethical or immoral act is never a focus on the self of the perpetrator, but on the use of another. Unethical behavior always makes the immoral person's goals dependent on the behavior or the being of the other. The critical issue of morality, therefore, is not how one focuses on another but how one focuses on oneself, and the byword should be: 'I will strive not to make my own salvation dependent on the functioning (no less the existence) of another'"[20] Making our salvation dependent on others shows a lack of self-differentiation.

On the other hand, the self is important. Can we think of self in terms of integrity, not narcissism or autocracy? Friedman suggested that if you are going to deal with the pathogenic forces in this world, you have to have a healthy dose of self.[21]

Friedman offered the idea that the concept of differentiation leads to a concept of the self that is moral. The Bowenian notion is of a self that is connected, never a cut-off self, but also never an invasive self. So the self can pursue its own development, but will automatically not be invasive and destructive of others.[22]

Friedman said that the major issue in differentiation is one's own values and goals. Once again, the basic philosophy/ theology should be that I will not make my salvation dependent on others. I will take maximum responsibility for my functioning. What keeps the focus on self moral is accountability — to myself if not to others. This moves away from blaming others and toward taking responsibility for my own being and destiny. With this approach, it is less likely that one will be invasive and thus harmful of others.[23]

The notion of differentiation says that togetherness, to be worth anything, depends on the self of the partners. Both must have self in order for a mature relationship to exist.

Where my own thinking has been headed with this lately has to do with "doing good," "helping others," and the question of invasiveness. This is related to the notion of the overfunctioning/underfunctioning reciprocity, in which both the "overfunctioner," the person taking too much responsibility, and the "under-functioner," the person taking not enough responsibility, lack self. Neither is able to determine what is most important for themselves and follow a clear direction forward.

The overfunctioner is just as dependent on the underfunctioner as the underfunctioner is dependent on the overfunctioner. They in fact are both immature and unable to have a mature focus on self.

Reflecting on these concepts, and on my own experience as an overfunctioner (like most clergy) has brought me to the question: Is much of the "good" we do overfunctioning? Overfunctioning involves getting in the space of another. It involves being convinced that I know what is right for someone else. Overfunctioners believe that no one else can do it as well as they can. That sounds to me suspiciously like the sin of pride.

Paul's image of the body of Christ may provide some help. He says, "The eye cannot say to the hand, 'I have no need of you,' nor again the head to the feet, 'I have no need of you.' On the contrary, the members of the body that seem to be weaker are indispensable..." (I Cor. 12:21). The body of Christ provides an image of individuals who are connected together, each responsible for his or her own functioning, and ultimately to Christ as the Head.

For me to suggest that I know what is best for others is to usurp their function and limit their functioning. It also keeps me from focusing on myself and on my own functioning. If I spend all my time doing "good" things for others, I don't have to pay attention to myself. And I may get a lot of attention from others for my "good" works, too! If the nature of evil is invasive, as Friedman suggests, and overfunctioning is invasive, what does that say about much of the "good" we do?

Let's go back for a moment to the two organisms in the study mentioned earlier. As the organisms were moved closer and closer, the smaller organism began to disintegrate and was destroyed. There was no hostile attack, but the proximity of these two organisms without immune systems (without self) was enough to destroy the smaller.

One human being can destroy another with hostile intent, and we can clearly call that evil. One human being can also destroy another without hostile intent, if each one lacks self. Perhaps this is truly "killing with kindness." The overfunctioning one in effect absorbs the other. We can see the extreme case in the parent who will not allow a child to mature, and continues to make decisions for the child and protects the child from the world. We can agree on the destructive aspect of this way of functioning.

But as Bowen described it, differentiation is a continuum. What about the less extreme cases? In family life, in terms of traditional roles, we all know the husband who takes all the responsibility for finances, or the wife who takes all the responsibility for parenting. Each is keeping his or her spouse from developing in those areas, from learning to function there.

If I am keeping someone from growing by my overfunctioning (and, incidentally, distracting myself from my own growth), am I not hurting them, and myself? Is that not ethically questionable? The immature cell/person/organization lacks self-regulation. When we rush in to help someone, we are often acting in an un-self-regulated manner. Our own anxiety causes us to want to do something — not because we really have a sense of what is best, but because we lack the maturity to sit back and wait.

Susan Luff, a therapist and R.N. who worked with Edwin Friedman in his training program for clergy, argues that while helping is thought to be altruistic, helping often is not truly for others' benefit. It is really for ourselves and our need to avoid our own anxiety. She said, "Helping can be selfish," and quoted Alan Watts: "Kindly let me help you before you drown, as he placed the fish safely up in the tree."[24]

Friedman related altruism to self-regulation.[25] Anxious helping is not altruistic, and often does not "help" at all. It does not lead to growth, but to dependency.

I do not mean to say that all helping is invasive and unethical or that we should immediately stop doing good things for people. I do mean to ask whether challenge can be as good as "help." Perhaps holding people accountable can be more helpful than doing good things for them. Yet humility is also appropriate as we relate to people, even when we think we know best. Perhaps if we get out of their way, they can come up with creative solutions to their problems that we never even dreamed of. Even if these solutions are not as "effective" as ours, those involved will be better off for having created and applied them.

We may find it hard to imagine that what we have thought of as "good" behavior can potentially be harmful to others. I have found that using this approach involves a reframing of the mind, a new way of thinking.

Can Bowen's concept of differentiation help us as we seek to live mature and ethical lives? Remember that differentiation of self involves a focus on self, a clarity about one's own purpose and values, yet remaining connected to others. Being a self, being connected — these are the twin aspects of differentiation.

If I am a self, with clear boundaries, I am less likely to invade others and take advantage of their boundaries. Yet I will not withdraw in selfish isolation. I will remain engaged with others. In this way I can make a difference — not by anxiously running around trying to fix everything and everyone, but by the nature of my better-differentiated presence in the emotional system. This is true whether I am relating to my family, my congregation, my denomination or the society at large.

The focus on self is not selfish, because our "self," who we are, is God-given. And the more I mature myself, the more I will be able to call others to maturity. Jesus himself said "Love your neighbor as yourself" (Mark 12:31). To follow this command to love, we must be a self.

This approach to ethics is different from a rule book approach. There is no magic "technique" for ethical behavior toward others, no list of do's and don'ts. "It's not what you do, but how you do it," was another favorite Friedman aphorism. If I "help" someone, anxiously assuming it is my responsibility to solve their problem, I will probably do more harm than good. If I offer a helping hand with the notion that the responsibility for their lives is theirs alone, and with a relaxed sensibility about it, perhaps I am indeed helping. If I know when to offer challenge, that too can be a "help." The philosopher Friedrich Nietzsche once said that a good friend is like a hard bed.[26]

While Bowen theory may be relatively new on the scene, similar insights have been understood through the ages. Two medieval writers, as interpreted in the modern era, may offer us some guidance in this matter. Joan Chittister, writing about St. Benedict's guidelines for abbots and prioress of Benedictine communities, suggests an approach for leaders that makes room for challenge as well as support, and which does not foster dependency. She points out: "Benedict wants a community that is led, but not driven. The concept is clear: people are not acquitted of the responsibility for their own souls. Personal decisions are still decisions, personal judgments are still judgments, free will is still free will. Being in a family does not relieve a child of the responsibility to grow up. The function of twenty-one-year-olds is not to do life's tasks as their parents told them to when they were six years old. The function of twenty-one-year-olds is simply to do the same tasks well and to take accountability themselves for having done them....The role of leadership is not to make lackeys or foot soldiers or broken children out of adult Christians."[27]

Each of us must ultimately find our own way. It is irresponsible and arrogant to presume to know that way for another. Sometimes we can be the most "help" by giving people space to find creative solutions to their own struggles. Sometimes, to do good is to do nothing while remaining emotionally present and connected to people.

Gerald May discusses the ideas of St. John of the Cross under the title "Don't Be a Pest." Four hundred years ago John offered advice to spiritual directors of people who were moving toward deeper awareness of God, and were in distress as a result. John said directors often know only how to "hammer and pound" with practices and concepts that "they themselves have used or read of somewhere," these "pestiferous" directors work against the exquisite gift God is giving.

May uses this example from John of the Cross: "Images and perceptions of God disappear. A person might say, 'God used to be very real for me as a loving Presence, but now all I find is emptiness and void." Spiritual directors may desperately want to help fill this void, but John says it would be a mistake to try to do so.... Putting it succinctly, he says, 'God does not fit in an occupied heart"[28]

Real spiritual implications exist in our overfunctioning, our getting in the space of others. What could be more ethically questionable than interfering in someone's relationship with God? I must plead guilty as I think of the times I have been made so anxious by someone's spiritual crisis that I wanted to do something, anything, to make it better.

Friedman suggested in *Generation to Generation,* "One of the subtlest yet most fundamental effects of overfunctioning is spiritual. It destroys the spiritual quality of the overfunctioner. Several ministers and rabbis have reported, after switching professions: 'Now I can go back to being a good Christian/Jew; now I can enjoy prayers and the Holy Days again.'"[29]

"Don't be a pest" may be my new watchword as a pastor! Isn't it more commendable to respect people's capabilities than to assume I know best? Even as a parent, there are times when I will do my children more good by giving them space, by "getting small" as Friedman once put it, than by a conviction that I always know best under every circumstance from birth to age 18 (and beyond!).[30]

For those of us with a lifetime of practice in pestering others to let us do things for their own good, this new framework is not easy. We may feel deep within us that this approach is cold, unfeeling, unchristian — unethical, that not helping is bad. We are programmed to help. Those of us who enter professional ministry are probably as thoroughly programmed as anyone! But can we learn to trust God with the lives of others?

When I can overcome the feelings I've described, that is, my own anxious need to be helpful, I find greater freedom and creativity in my own response to people, and greater response on their part. I have found this to be true in my own family, in individuals I've worked with, and with the congregation as a whole.

Being too serious can be a liability in this process. Taking responsibility for everything and everyone is a very serious position. Being good (ethical) and being serious are not identical. A light touch can go a long way toward clarifying what we do and don't need to do for others. In order to have this relaxed and light touch, we need to have a sense of security. That security can come from faith. If we live out of trust in God, we can relax — we don't have to worry about taking care of everyone, because all the results do not depend on us.

Perhaps Jesus can be our model here. I remember reading *The Humor of Christ* , by Elton Trueblood, as a teenager, and finding the idea revolutionary that Jesus had a sense of humor. Jesus as portrayed in the gospels gives people space, and makes space for himself. Jesus, more than anyone else, was able to live out of a position of relaxed trust. He simply said, "Your sins are forgiven. Go and sin no more."

Paul says in Philippians 2:12, "Work out your own salvation with fear and trembling..." As a leader, he is telling his readers to obey him, while acknowledging that the responsibility for their lives is ultimately their own. Elsewhere he wrote, "Bear one another's burdens and so fulfill the law of Christ." (Galatians 6:2). How can we obey both these injunctions? As we mature, emotionally and in the faith, we are better able to deal with tension and ambiguity. Should we bear someone's burdens or challenge them to work out their salvation? It depends! Don't be a pest!

NOTES

[1]Edwin H. Friedman, *Generation to Generation: Family Process in Church and Synagogue* (New York: Guilford Press, 1985), p. 27.

[2]Ibid., pp. 27-28.

[3]Michael Kerr & Murray Bowen, *Family Evaluation* (W. W. Norton & Company, 1988), p. 68.

[4]Alan S. Gurman and David Kniskern, eds., *Handbook of Family Therapy*, Vol. 2. (New York: runner/Mazel, 1991), p. 143.

[5]Ibid., p. 144.

[6]Friedman, *Generation to Generation*, pp. 23-27.

[7]Gurman and Kniskern, *Handbook of Family Therapy*, p. 144.

[8]Kerr & Bowen, *Family Evaluation*, p. 55.

[9]Ibid.

[10]Ibid., p. 55-56.

[11]Ibid., pp. 73-75.

[12]Ibid., p. 113.

[13]Ibid., p. 114.

[14]Gurman and Kniskern, p. 140.

[15]Ibid., p. 156.

[16]Ibid.

[17]Edwin H. Friedman, lecture, May 29, 1996.

[18]Ibid.

[19]Edwin H. Friedman, *Family Process and Process Theology.* Alban Institute, 1991. Videocassette.

[20]Ibid.

[21]Ibid.

[22]Ibid.

[23]Friedman, lecture, September 19, 1996.

[24]Luff, Susan. "Overfunctioning Leadership Gone Awry." Lecture presented at the Postgraduate Clergy Seminar in Family Emotional Process, Bethesda, Maryland, October 26, 1995.

[25]Friedman, lecture, May 29, 1996.

[26]Friedrich Nietzsche, *Thus Spoke Zarathustra* (Penguin Classics 1961).

[27]Chittister, Joan. *The Rule of Benedict* (New York: Crossroad, 1992), p. 38.

[28]Gerald May, "Don't Be a Pest," *Shalem News,* Vol. 21, No. 2 (Summer 1997), p 5.

[29]Friedman, *Generation to Generation,* p. 212.

[30]Friedman, *Family Process and Process Theology.*

III
REFRAMING
MINISTRY CONTEXT

12

Reframing the Congregation

Rebecca Maccini

W hy did rabbi, therapist, and author Edwin Friedman, whose writing and workshops have influenced thousands of clergy, describe the clergy as the eyes of the congregation? It's because clergy are in a unique position, having access to and observing committees, task forces, teams, groups, boards, and ministries of the congregation. In their pastoral role, clergy have a unique perspective on what is happening in the families in the congregation; and, as worship leaders, they have a view from the front of the sanctuary, where they are face to face with those sitting in the congregation and also have a view of those attending through platforms like Zoom. From their position in a congregation, clergy are uniquely positioned to reframe a congregation.

I agreed to be hired by a congregation to "build community and increase membership." In a short time, I recognized that this was an overwhelming responsibility for one person. I sought insight from a wise pastoral counselor who told me that the pastor's job is to witness to the congregation. His advice did not encompass the range of responsibilities that I saw as essential to pastoral ministry, nor did it match the congregation's stated purpose for which I had been hired. However, the counselor did not mean that witnessing to the congregation involved giving up visiting and connecting with them, preaching, teaching, serving sacraments, and praying—responsibilities essential to the pastor's job description. Rather, he meant that a primary task, amidst the essentials of the job description, is to develop competent skill in observing a congregation and sharing those observations with them.

What tools are available to clergy to make themselves better observers? Bowen Family Systems Theory (BFST) provides a framework through which to view congregational patterns of operating, patterns that are central pieces in the puzzle of an honest description of how the congregation functions. Dynamics in one's family strongly influence how one interacts with others, makes decisions, acts in relationships, and participates in a congregation.

In science, the observer effect states that when we observe things, those things change. As a clergy person who observes a congregation, I am in the role that can be a catalyst for change, for myself, certainly. Keen observation may also elicit change in a congregation. The framework from which I observe and what I share influence the responses and actions of the congregation. Reframing or understanding of a congregation begins with observing and asking questions that begin with who, when, what, where, and how about the unique culture (worship, education, identity, language, purpose), context, and history of that congregation.[1]

The clergyperson is not the only individual that observes a congregation. Anyone may do so, but their view will be from a quite different framework and will, generally, be geared toward whatever specific task, ministry, or committee they are invested in: a choir, the trustees, youth ministry, to name just a few. The lens of BFST seeks a view from the balcony, a "psychological vantage point from which to view others," and a place from which to observe oneself and one's biases while obtaining some space to reflect upon what's going on.[2]

Congregations have the same overarching mission: to be an expression of the Church, which is the mystery of God's purposes and love enacted in the world. Each congregation has a distinct understanding of their unique mission and ministry, an understanding shaped by the congregation's individual culture. The words in Acts 2:42–47, often referred to as the marks of the church, prescribe actions in the lives of congregations: worship, communion, proclamation, prayer, fellowship, teaching, and outreach. Every congregation demonstrates some or all of these marks, but each congregation will convey them with distinct variety, color, expression, and quantity.

Researching a Congregation

Researching a congregation's history, especially how it began, will gather information and answer who, when, what, where, and how questions. The answers to these questions lead to the discovery of facts about the functioning of a congregation. While researching, one learns about patterns of functioning in a congregation. One begins by looking at the founding of a congregation—the early documents, the reasons for being, the historical players, the challenges and issues present at the organization of a congregation and the resources of the congregation to meet initial challenges.

At a congregation's beginning, someone stepped up and wrote a check to cover unpaid buildings costs. Throughout its fifty-year history, a pattern emerged that whenever the congregation was in trouble financially, someone would "save" the budget by writing a check to cover the expenses. Because the income covered the expenses at the end of the year, the congregation never paid attention to the how budget was rescued, and few in leadership positions thought about how income matched expenses until one year when a large deficit erupted. The leaders immediately began to ponder which expenses to cut, and they decided that the quick fix was to eliminate financial support for the wider denomination, even though the congregation was known for its strong denominational ties. The blowback came swiftly. A group of people threatened to leave the church if giving to the denomination was cut.

The pastor, now curious about giving patterns, started asking questions, and discovered that the overfunctioning of a "financial savior" occurred regularly over the life of the congregation. The pastor sought out the individual who was the current manifestation of the financial savior. It turned out that this person had gotten a divorce and was no longer able to give copiously as in recent years. When the pastor brought the dynamic of the financial savior to the attention of the church leaders, it became clear to them that the congregation had been neglectful in attending to healthier stewardship of finances. The discovery of the facts about the finances resulted in the squelching of the blame and misinterpretation that had begun and provided more accurate information for decision-making.

A budget is, of course, one issue in a congregation that gets attention and triggers people's anxiety. However, it is just one of many other issues that are attention grabbers and anxiety provokers—among them, for example, music styles, youth programs, and the use and maintenance of buildings. Instead of engaging with such issues, one can ask questions and think about the functioning and patterns of functioning in the congregation. Who gets to make decisions: one person, a few people, a committee? Are they made through the path outlined in the by-laws or through an informal path? Are decisions made during official meetings or in the parking lot following the meeting? The answers to such questions present more accurate information and factual picture of a congregation emerges to clarify strengths, weaknesses, opportunities and threats.

Congregations formulate church vision statements as expressions of where they want to go. Their words are uplifting and hopeful: to make a lasting difference; to see people set free to serve and be empowered; to alleviate suffering; to be people transformed by Jesus; to be extravagantly welcoming. The words are idealistic expressions of the intentions of a congregation. Dynamics in congregations exist that inhibit or catalyze, move congregations off course or help them maintain or create a course. The same dynamics influence the functioning of individuals, boards, and committees that make and carry out decisions.

Congregations have reputations. Dioceses, synods, conferences, and associations know which congregations are "plum," generally those whose clergy have long pastorates and where there is minimal crises; and which are "pill," those that experience frequent conflict and whose pastors are regularly "spit . . . out after a few years."[3] It is as if each congregation has a particular pattern that affects how it operates.

Congregations are not families, yet the same relationship dynamics exist between members and friends in a congregation as exist in a family. We learn how to be in relationship with other people from the families in which we grew up. We are imbued with lessons, many unconscious, about what constitutes connection with another person, what it means to be close, who gets to speak and when, where authority rests, when and what to fear. Families have themes—for example, peace at any price; mom wears the pants in the family; and you're not the boss of me. Individuals, without thinking, carry these themes and adapt them, depending upon the context, into their adult lives, the families they create, work environments, and congregations.[4]

Overfocussing on Issues

A new hymnal was introduced into a progressive denomination, the United Church of Christ, forty years after its organization. Along with many new songs, the hymnal also introduced changes to words of common hymns and removed the word "Lord," substituting "God." One church leader, whose family theme was "There is one right way," focused upon the "Lord" issue. She posted in the church building and public places around town an article from a popular national magazine that denigrated the new hymnal. She saw no value in the congregation hosting meetings to discuss what was important to people about hymns, no virtue in singing a new song, nor did she consider what might be gained by embracing the new hymnal.

Although a conversation about the hymnal did occur eventually, her preemptive actions and intense focus on the "Lord" issue that had been broadcast in the congregation and the wider community sabotaged the process and resulted in a narrow conversation. The primary focus of the congregation on the issue of the removal of "Lord" demonstrated not so much a theological stance as a penchant for a quick fix of an issue whose resolution would be time-consuming and almost certainly involve conflict because strong differences of opinion would be voiced.

Togetherness and Individuality

Every person possesses two instincts that strongly impact the functioning of a congregation. One instinct is togetherness, the propensity to want to connect with others and belong. Togetherness is a spectrum, and the stronger it is, the more it will have the appearance of being alike, agreeing with, or standing with others and their beliefs and values. The other instinct is individuality: figuring out what one believes and feels and acting for oneself. An example of early human togetherness is people developing a tribe and hunting together because a group had a greater survival rate than an individual had. Individuality is like the song "I've Gotta Be Me." Togetherness and individuality are counterbalancing instincts that function at the same time. What enables me, or any person, to develop maturity in relationships is to remain connected and have a sense of belonging while determining my own beliefs and values and taking responsibility for my decisions and actions.

Togetherness instincts increase when a threat is real or perceived and anxiety arises. When an immediate fear (acute anxiety), real or perceived, or when a fear of what might be, real or perceived, is ongoing (chronic anxiety), togetherness may be so strong that a "herd instinct" ensues, and this suppresses individuality.[5] When a threat for survival is perceived in a congregation—which has become common in congregations since the onset of Covid-19 as the threat that a congregation will not continue because young families are absent from the community—a group will act as a herd with the same thoughts and feelings and will blame something for the threat. One example is a Women's Fellowship in a congregation that claimed that parents were not bringing their children to Sunday school because the teachers were not teaching "orthodox doctrine" to children. Nothing the teachers did—putting the children's biblically based work on the walls, doing skits about Bible stories in worship— made any difference in the eyes of the Women's Fellowship.

A couple of congregations I have served have had a sign in front of their meetinghouse: "All Are Welcome." Like a wonderfully crafted vision statement, a sign with those words portends good intentions. However, what makes a congregation welcoming is not words on a sign but rather its capacity to relate to others who have diverse views, ideas, and lifestyles. This is influenced by how the people of the congregation have managed differences of opinions, theologically, politically, and socially, both historically and currently. Does the congregation receive differences with grace and acceptance, compassion, curiosity and/or playfulness? Is there an illusion that differences do not exist, or are recognized differences demonized, or something in between? How does a congregation allow for individuality and/or how much togetherness is required?

Those who are part of a congregation have a common understanding of the vision, mission, and ministry of a congregation, a togetherness that allows the congregation to exist.[6] This common understanding encompasses espoused and assumed ways of functioning. Qualities of togetherness range from generosity of spirit to unspoken rules that are rigid and irreformable. A subgroup of a congregation—the choir, a group of women or of men, parents of youth—may hold a common understanding that is so strong that they choose, consciously or unconsciously, not to relate to or to denigrate others in the congregation whose beliefs vary from their own because they perceive the others as a threat to the stability of the congregation. An example is a group of congregation members who are part of a congregation for many years, who have family in the congregation, and who are unable to relate to, talk with, or work purposefully with those who are newer to the congregation, who bring with them other experiences and ideas to be considered for incorporation into the mission and ministry.

Congregations are formed for the purpose of being the Church; and congregations do not exist without relationships. An honest portrayal of a congregation occurs when factual who, what, when, and where questions are answered, and historical and current patterns of functioning are recognized. Patterns of functioning are also present in the families of individuals in the congregations, and individuals carry these patterns into their adult lives, impacting their relationships, actions, and behaviors. The patterns of functioning of members, friends, and clergy in the congregation interact with the historical functioning of the congregation. Reframing a congregation requires paying attention to how a congregation rises to challenges, and finding out who was involved, when it happened, what exactly happened, and what resources were engaged to meet the challenge. Every interaction between people in a congregation is more than a relationship between those who are present. Contributing to the interactions are familial relationships of the people, multigenerational family patterns of the people, and the history of relationship patterns in the congregation.

NOTES

[1]Summarized from Israel Galindo, *The Hidden Lives of Congregations: Understanding Congregational Dynamics* (Herndon, VA: Alban Institute, 2004), pp. 21–37.

[2]Ronald A. Heifetz, *Leadership Without Easy Answers* (Cambridge, MA: Belknap Press of Harvard University Press, 1994), p. 271.

[3]Edwin H. Friedman, Margaret M. Treadwell, and Edward W. Beal, eds., *A Failure of Nerve: Leadership in the Age of the Quick Fix* (New York: Seabury, 2007), p. 250.

[4]Israel Galindo, Elaine Boomer, Don Reagan, *A Family Genogram Workbook* (Educational Consultants, 2017), pp. 30ff.

[5]Friedman, Treadwell, and Beal, *A Failure of Nerve*, p. 67.

[6]Galindo, *The Hidden Lives of Congregations*, p. 2.

13

Reframing Togetherness

William T. Pyle

I have been fascinated by the dance that humans use to
navigate the tension between our intense need for
togetherness and our allergic reaction to too much of
it. I seemed like I was always struggling to find the right
balance of togetherness without feeling smothered. I also
recognized that what felt right to me was often at odds
with other people's experience. My comfort zone seldom
aligned with what other people wanted. I experienced
"their" comfort zone as either too distant or smothering.
Without a theoretical perspective, my experience was
bewildering.

My introduction to Bowen Family Systems has
provided a broader framework to thinking about these
vital instincts of togetherness and individuality, my need
to be connected to others and my need to be a self. I began
to think about the particular orientations toward life that I
inherited from my family of origin. This orientation
shaped the ways that I thought and reacted to other
people. Little by little, I began to turn my focus away from

getting closer to other people and toward getting clarity about my values and how I will choose to live my life. In this chapter, I will explore how developing more viable contact with my family provides an opportunity for personal growth. I think that the process of developing a clear and distinct "self" begins within the family of origin and continues as we navigate the balance of individuality and shared togetherness. While I will be thinking about togetherness and the way that I connect to other people, I will enter a side door. How does the way that we differentiate and separate from our family of origin shape the ways we are able to connect to other people? How does the process of emotional cutoff affect our ability to connect to others in significant ways?

One of the curiosities of Bowen Family Systems is the way that the concepts of the theory are interlocking. They fit together is such a way that you can begin to think about the theory using any of the eight concepts as an entry point. And any entry point can naturally lead to a discussion of any of the other concepts. In this chapter, I will be thinking about Emotional Cutoff. And while that will be my focus, I will be sliding into the discussion of other concepts as they relate to my focus. We will be thinking systems, so we will be thinking about the ways that all the concepts connect to this particular phenomenon.

When Dr. Bowen began to observe Nuclear Family Emotional Process, he identified a small number of predictable mechanisms that families typically use to navigate the push and pull of the togetherness and individuality instincts. He described these as emotional processes. By that he meant that they were instinctual and automatic. They operated behind and beyond conscious choices or decisions. The functional value of the mechanisms was that they provided enough space for the individual to carve out an individual identity. Often two partners use marital conflict, spousal dysfunction, or other distancing mechanisms to create the space and distance that they need to not feel smothered in their relationship. Sometimes the stress cannot be contained in the one generation and their anxiety is managed by focusing on a child.

Early on, Dr. Bowen included distance as one of the mechanisms, but over time it emerged as the overarching umbrella for the other mechanisms. Each of the mechanisms focus as a distancing maneuver that provides space for the individual to develop. As such, distancing is a critical survival skill. Distance provides the counterbalance to our intense need for togetherness. Both are essential for us to thrive as an individual, as a family, and as a society.

While Dr. Bowen first began to think of distancing as a mechanism operating within the nuclear family, he also observed the way that distancing operated between generations. Just as individuals need to find space in a marital relationship, children must find space to develop their own identity apart from their parents. The concept of Emotional Cutoff was one of the last concepts formally added to the theory even though he had been observing and writing about the phenomenon for years. I think that he included it as one of the eight concepts to call attention to the importance of creating identity apart from the family, and the challenge that comes from creating the necessary space without transferring the unresolved emotional attachment to other relationships. While distancing and cutoff are sometimes used as functional synonyms, I will use emotional cutoff to refer to the distancing that occurs when one separates from their family of origin.

I think that Dr, Bowen was clearest when he described the concept in his paper, "Theory in the Practice of Psychotherapy" that was included in *Family Therapy in Clinical Practice.* "The life pattern of cutoffs is determined by the way people handle their unresolved emotional attachments to their parents. All people have some degree of unresolved emotional attachment to their parents. The lower the level of differentiation, the more intense the unresolved attachment. The concept deals with the way people separate themselves from the past in order to start their lives in the present generation. Much thought went into the selection of a term to best describe this process of separation, isolation, withdrawal, running away, or denying the importance of the parental family."[1]

The process of emotional cutoff begins at birth and continues as the individual begins to think and act for self. It is a necessary and essential emotional process. One becomes a self through differentiating from others, primarily from parents. The gradual process of differentiating a self, looks and feels different for those who have a little more emotional maturity. For them it is more like an organic process of growing away. They gradually get clearer about what they think and who they will be. There is less reactivity to the family and their direction is being governed more by their values and clearest thinking. The emotional and physical distancing is toward something rather than running away from something. "In healthy, well-differentiated families, this difficult transition involves a gradual, yet steady, letting go on the part of the parents and a willingness on the part of the child to assume more personal responsibility."[2]

Peter Titelman describes the unfolding process of emotional separation between the adolescent or young adult and his or her parents this way, "At the highest level of functioning the process can be characterized in terms of an individual growing away from his or her family of origin, leading to the development of an autonomous self."[3] Those with less emotional maturity may experience something quite different. They may define themselves as over against the thinking of their family. Their efforts of differentiation may be threatening to the family and they are chastised for being different. The efforts to restrain their growth may seem so powerful that it feels like an existential threat--they must tear away to get away. The natural process of emotional cutoff is present in both scenarios, even if it is experienced quite differently for those involved. All people experience emotional cutoff as they separate from their family of origin and create a life of their own. It is a difference of degree rather a difference of kind.

Individuals create distance from their family of origin through the interpsychic process of emotional isolation or by physically distancing themselves from their parents. Most individuals combine both strategies of emotional isolation and physical distancing. The intense pull of the togetherness instinct is countered by these distancing mechanisms. My suspicion is that most of our distancing is beyond our conscious awareness. Individuals often imitate the distancing techniques that they have inherited from previous generations without thinking about how to be in close contact with significant others in meaningful ways. I think that Dr. Bowen recognized that unresolved emotional attachment to parents influenced the way that an individual handled the challenges of life and provided a prediction about how one would relate to other significant people in their life. "The more intense the cutoff with the past, the more likely the individual to have an exaggerated version of his parental family problem in his own marriage, and the more likely his own children to do a more intense cutoff with him in the next generation."[4]

Physical distance can be an attempt to gain emotional distance from one's family of origin. However one person can live half a continent away from his family of origin and maintain reasonably open relationships with many members of the family, while another person may live in the same house with parents and handles the attachment by emotional isolation. Physical distance is only one factor to be considered.

Michael Kerr described one kind of family system as "explosive." These families tend to scatter across the country, leaving people separated by geographic distance. "In better differentiated "explosive" families, people move apart in the process of pursuing life goals. Though physically distant, they maintain good emotional contact. In the poorly differentiated "explosive" families, people are getting away from one another. They are not only physically distant, but they are out of contact emotionally."[5] The other family system that Kerr described are more "cohesive" in nature. They tend to live in close physical proximity to one another for generations. Their physical proximity is no more an indication of healthy emotional closeness than physical distance is an indicator of emotional cutoff. "In the better differentiated "cohesive" families, people are fairly involved in one another's lives and, for the most part, in comfortable emotional contact. In the poorly differentiated "cohesive" families, people may interact with one another regularly, but the level of emotional reactivity is often sufficiently high that people are isolated emotionally even though they are in contact physically."[6] It appears to me that the level of differentiation in the family and the level of viable emotional contact between the members are the keys to the extent that unresolved emotional attachment will limit the trajectory of a life. Kerr did not offer an opinion on whether explosive or cohesive family patterns were to be desired or promoted. I think that the level of viable emotional contact is more important than geographic distance.

People who seek to escape the intensity of the relationship with their family of origin through physical distance often find themselves replicating the relationship dynamics in their new location. Dr. Bowen made this observation, "The one who runs away geographically is more inclined to impulsive behavior. He tends to see the problem as being the parents and running away as a method of gaining independence from the parents. The more intense the cutoff, the more he is vulnerable to duplicating the pattern with parents with the first available person. He can get into an impulsive marriage.

When problems develop in the marriage, he tends also to run away from that."[7]

While Dr. Bowen talked about the marriage as the primary place when unresolved emotional process would show up; he also mentioned "substitute families" as places where these dynamics might manifest. I wonder how unresolved emotional process from families of origin might show up in congregational dynamics. What would it look like when a pastoral leader expects his or her congregation to provide what they missed in their family of origin? Or could the unrealistic expectation of some congregants be based on unresolved emotional process from their family of origin? One assumption of the theory is that emotional cutoff is a given in every family. If that is true, every congregation is composed of individuals who bring their unresolved emotional processes with them. Substitute families and outside relationships are poor substitutes for working out unresolved issues with the family of origin.

One common misunderstanding of Bowen's use of the term "emotional cutoff" is the tendency to hear it pejoratively as a diagnosis to be cured, or to hear it as a label for "some" families. I think all families have some degree of emotional cutoff. All families could benefit by more members working to stay in viable emotional contact with one another in less reactive ways. This broader understanding of emotional cutoff moves beyond diagnosis and blaming to thinking about how to increase meaningful contact with extended family. Any successful effort that goes toward improving the frequency and quality of emotional contact with the extended family will predictably improve their family's capacity to deal with the challenges of life and reduce symptoms in the nuclear family.

One way of thinking about emotional cutoff is to recognize the variety of ways that distance occurs within families. Peter Titelman offers examples that illustrate the various forms that emotional cutoff may manifest.

1. A young adult (or any family member) not communicating with other family when geographically distant, particularly avoiding communicating bad news
2. Being conflictual with a family member prior to embarking on a separation from that person
3. An individual's polarizing his or her position with a parent in order to gain emotional distance
4. Forgetting or choosing not to acknowledge important events or milestones such as birthdays, anniversaries, graduations, or achievements
5. The absence or refusal to make eye contact with the other
6. The absence or avoidance of verbal communication with the other
7. Not referring to the other by name

8. Not initiating contact, but responding to it, or not initiating and not responding to contact from the other.[8]

These are examples of what Titelman refers to as manifestations of primary cutoff or direct cutoff. They ordinarily happen within the primary triangle of an individual and one or both parents. While the concept originally focused on the primary triangle, the natural progression is that the emotional cutoff in one generation is often perpetuated through following generations.

Titelman calls these "indirect" or "inherited" cutoffs. They are inherited in the sense that an individual has little or no contact with extended family members because of cutoff in previous generations. With little contact, it is difficult to develop a one-on-one relationship with some of the extended family members. I think that one of the benefits of a family diagram is the opportunity to become curious about those parts of the family I know little about. That can provide an opportunity to begin bridging the secondary cutoff that I inherited. Each person that I develop a personal relationship with gradually diminishes the level and intensity of the cutoff that I inherited. I will either perpetuate or I will diminish the intensity of the cutoff that I inherited.

Dr. Bowen insisted that a family therapist usually had the very same problems in his or her own families that were present in the families that they saw professionally. He deduced that the therapist had an individual responsibility to define self in their own family if they were going to function effectively in their professional context. While the minister functions in a different context and emotional system than the therapist, the principle applies. The emotional processes at work in the congregation and the congregational families will reflect the emotional processes in my family. To the extent that I can define a self while staying in viable emotional contact with my extended family, I am better prepared to be a resource to the congregations where I minister.

The concluding chapter in Edwin Friedman's book, *Generation to Generation*, is titled "Extended Family: Potential for Salvation." He summarized his thesis this way, "A major theme of this work has been the significance of anyone's family of origin for his or her functioning in other systems. It has been emphasized throughout that not only does our position in our extended families affect how we function in other relationships, but also that efforts to gain better differentiation of self in that extended field will have corresponding effects at home, at work, and on our health."[9] Bowen Family Systems Theory applies these principles to all humans, regardless of race, ethnicity, or gender. Friedman was concerned with the particular application of these principles to clergy. The work of bridging emotional cutoff and increasing differentiation of self, increases our capacity to sustain appropriate emotional contact with our congregational systems. The ability to define a self while staying in viable emotional contact with my extended family increases my capacity to be emotional present in my congregational family. This is how Edwin Friedman applied this process to clergy, "Generally speaking, anyone who works to gain more differentiation of self in his or her family of origin will find that the way one thinks and functions within his or her vocation is affected. This is because in the process of becoming better defined, we become clearer about life's goals."[10]

For the clergy, however the connection is deeper and more direct. There is no other profession on this planet where the ideals, the values, the principles, and the professional commitment are so much part and parcel of one's work...Since beliefs are the essence of self, to the extent we work to gain differentiation in our families of origin, we directly affect the context of our professional existence."[11] I think that this process of becoming better defined is affected by the amount and intensity of the emotional cutoffs that remain from our separating from our family of origin. The unresolved emotional issues around our separation tend to be displaced into the new relationships that we enter. Cutoff engenders both more intensity and more sensitivity to the unresolved emotional issues from my family of origin as they show up in my congregation. My best chance at being able to emotional connect with parishioners in healthy ways is directly connected to my ability to connect to members of my extended family. If I want to navigate the balance of togetherness and individuality in my congregational context, I will work at bridging cutoff in my family of origin.

For me, this reframing of the togetherness and individuality instincts has lead me back to my family of origin. I acknowledge that the level and intensity of the cutoff in my family of origin was mild compared to the emotional cutoff that other people experience. But it was a difference of degree rather than difference of kind. Most of the cutoff in my family was the result of benign neglect. I failed to acknowledge the importance of my extended family and neglected to continue the process of building emotionally viable one-on-one relationships.

In 2001, I began a slow and constant process of beginning to bridge some of the cutoffs in my extended family. For the past twenty years, I have been involved with continuing education programs that include family of origin work as an important part. I have used family systems coaching to help me identify places where I wanted to develop more viable contact. I have become more curious about the parts of my family tree that I knew little about. I have worked to develop individual

relationships with each of my siblings. I am now more
intentional about showing up at important family events.
One resource that I have found helpful was *A Family
Genogram Workbook.*[12] The exercises in the book provide a
guide for understanding your family and how it shaped
you.

Ronald Richardson's excellent book, *Becoming a
Healthier Pastor,* was helpful in describing this process of
developing a self by working on our unresolved emotional
attachment. He stated, "Our development and experience
within our family of origin is a major but usually hidden
component of how we function emotionally within our
congregations as pastors. The family we grew up in is the
first, most powerful, longest lasting, and nearly indelible
training we get for how to be a part of a group and to
function within it. While our later professional training
adds a layer of sophistication and expertise that normally
serves us well in ministry, when the level of anxiety goes
up in a congregation and we become anxious, we tend to
revert to our old family patterns and ways of
functioning."[13] The thesis of the book is that ministers who
can work on themselves within their family of origin will
have the best chance of becoming a healthier pastor and
more effective as a leader in their congregation. More
recently, Richardson has published a memoir that
describes his process of bridging cutoff in his family. It is a
fascinating window into one individual's journey.[14]

(Ronald Richardson, Mothers and Sons: Changing the Script)

While my stated title for this chapter is "Reframing Togetherness," I have spent most of the chapter talking about cutoff instead of togetherness. I now believe that my ability to experience closeness in relationships is enhanced by my work to define myself within my family of origin. As I navigate the balance between togetherness and individuality in my family of origin with openness, authenticity, and lower reactivity, I bring fewer unresolved emotional issues to my congregational setting. I am better able to show up, be authentically present, be my best self, and do my best work.

NOTES:

[1]Murray Bowen, *Family Therapy in Clinical Practice* (Jason Aronson, Inc., 1993), p. 382.
[2]"Congregational Life Dynamics and Conflict Management," UUA p. 37.
[3] Peter Titelman, *Emotional Cutoff: Bowen Family Systems Theory Perspectives* (Routledge, 2003), p. 24.
[4]Murray Bowen, *Family Therapy in Clinical Practice*, p. 382.
[5]Murray Bowen and Michael Kerr, *Family Evaluation* (W. W. Norton & Company, 1988), p. 274.
[6]Ibid., p. 274.
[7]Bowen, *Family Therapy in Clinical Practice*, p. 383.
[8]Titelman, *Emotional Cutoff*, pp. 24-25.
[9]Edwin H. Friedman, *Generation to Generation*, pp. 295-296.

[10]Ibid., p. 296.

[11]Ibid.

[12]Israel Galindo, Elaine Boomer, and Don Reagan, *A Family Genogram Workbook* (Educational Consultants, 2017).

[13]Ronald Richardson, *Becoming a Healthier Pastor* (Fortress Press, 2004), p. ix.

[14]Ronald Richardson, *Mothers and Sons: Changing the Script* (Independently Published, 2022).

14
Reframing Conflict:
The Hidden Potential of Conflict

Carla Toenniessen and Austin Almaguer

Conflict. Just hearing the word can stir up a sense of negativity, caution, and dread. And rightly so. The Merriam-Webster Dictionary defines conflict as "a clashing or sharp disagreement as between ideas, interests, or purposes." Conflict can refer to a fight or battle. There is even a term for dodging conflict at all costs, conflict avoidance. As I read the Bowen Theory literature, I am curious about the usefulness of conflict in the hands of a differentiated leader, both in a family, organization, or congregation. In this chapter, we will explore the hidden potential of conflict as a source of growth, creativity, dynamic action, and transformational power for congregations. What are the root causes of conflict in relationships and congregations? How does differentiated leadership limit the negative and maximize the positive effects of conflict? What are the positive outcomes of conflict when orchestrated into healthy disagreement and debate?

We live in a world full of variation and diversity, in nature and in people. Celebrating our differences makes life more meaningful and enjoyable and can be the foundation of a productive exchange of ideas. Yet it is those same differences that tend to stand out more when anxiety is high, leading to opposition that could erupt into hostile conflict.

Using the framework of Bowen Theory can provide information about the emotional process swirling behind the scenes of conflict. Emotional conflict is one of the ways humans use to manage anxiety and control the intensity that occurs from a lack of emotional differentiation in relationships. Differentiation is the ability to bring who I am to my relationships, to be clear about what I think, what I believe, what I value, and be true to my principles and goals while staying in emotional contact with others. According to Murray Bowen, "A 'differentiated self' is one who can maintain emotional objectivity while in the midst of an emotional system in turmoil, yet at the same time actively relate to key people in the system."[1]

In his book, *Bowen Theory's Secrets: Revealing the Hidden Life of Families*, Michael Kerr considers conflict as "not inherently bad." An exchange between people can air differences and viewpoints that fosters better understanding and clarity. Kerr points out that it is when conflict becomes emotional and reactive and a patterned way of responding in a system that it becomes problematic. When people are no longer dealing with facts, resort to blaming, and respond with reactivity rather than through thinking and reflection. According to Kerr, "Conflict arises from neither person having enough 'self' not to feel that going along with the other's wants and ideas is 'giving in'. The mutual defensiveness precludes reasoned compromise and cooperation. Poorly differentiated relationships are vulnerable to the most extreme levels of conflict."[2]

The Dynamics of Conflict

Looking closer at the dynamics of conflict, Bowen Theory identifies two variables: the degree of anxiety and the level of differentiation of self. For example, conflict is a symptom of increased anxiety and lower level of differentiation. Other dynamics include sensitivity to differences, individuality and togetherness forces, and triangles.[3]

Chronic anxiety. Anxiety is a natural part of life. Acute anxiety is a reaction to a real threat, wherein chronic anxiety results as a reaction to an imagined threat. People with a lower level of differentiation tend to be more susceptible to reacting to increased stressors and anxiety. Anxiety is contagious, but so is calm and thoughtful functioning.

Low level of maturity and differentiation. The level of differentiation is one of the two variables of Bowen Theory. Differentiation is key to a person's ability to manage self when anxiety increases.

Sensitivity to differences. People with less maturity and differentiation tend to be driven by dependency and a need for closeness. Normal disagreements can feel threatening and with increased discomfort a person may become reactive. As anxiety rises, differences tend to stand out even more, creating fertile ground for conflict.

Individuality and togetherness instincts. Bowen wrote about two inherent forces or instincts in life; individuality and togetherness. As a person matures, there is a natural drive towards autonomy and independence, exhibited by behaviors such as enjoying being alone, making choices, having preferences and goals, maintaining boundaries, and defining self. It is a natural part of human development and begins early in life. The togetherness instinct is the urge to move closer towards others to be together, to share interests, to find a sense of belonging and support. However, when anxiety increases so does the drive for more togetherness, sameness, to be part of the group. Out of this herding impulse, alliances and triangles can form, creating opposing factions and increased reactivity and emotionality that can disrupt the ability to think and function well.

Triangles. Triangles occur when poorly managed anxiety rises between two people causing the focus to move to a third party as an attempt to lower the intensity. Kathleen Smith, faculty member at the Bowen Center for the Study of the Family, describes triangles as what happens when tension between people builds and "spills over into relationships. We pull people into the conflict, wanting allies, confidantes, and messengers."[4]

Conflict in Congregations

Conflict is a part of life and can be found wherever people gather; whether in a family, a marriage, social group, or in an organization such as a congregation. The nature of congregations creates a natural breeding ground for conflict as religious groups tend to foster fusion and uniformity out of their mission of being loving and caring rather than supporting the deeper unity that honors individuality and differences. This culture of peace at any price increases sensitivity to any kind of disagreement. Rather than the expression of different viewpoints that could lead to constructive dialogue and understanding, alliances and polarization can create a climate of we versus they, described by pastor and consultant Peter Steinke in his book, *Congregational Leadership in Anxious Times.* According to Steinke, "A congregation's balance is disturbed more by people's strong reaction to one another than by reaction to the issues or the event itself. Conflict is no longer a time for learning but for conquering. Domination supplants education. Civility and courtesy give way to sneers and shouting."[5]

Conflict Avoidance

Conflict avoidance can also exacerbate the situation by covering up necessary issues that can fester and keep the congregation stuck and dysfunctional. Underneath the avoidance lies anxiety and fear both real and imagined, fear of disrupting relationships, fear of reprisal, fear of negative consequences, and fear of the unknown. What might happen if I brought up this issue? For thousands of years, humans have relied on the family group and each other for finding food and shelter, withstanding hardship and danger, and surviving matters of life and death. Who would want to upset the necessary safety net of relationships and patterned community life? What is the way through? It takes differentiated leadership to chart the course and help mature the system.

Differentiated Leadership

The degree of poorly managed anxiety in a system and in people contributes to the potential for conflict and polarization. However, the second variable, the capacity for differentiation in the system, can make the difference in whether conflict becomes disruptive or used to promote growth and learning. In their book *Family Evaluation,* Michael Kerr and Murray Bowen offer a description of this kind of differentiated leadership. They list traits of a family leader which could be the leader of any group whether a family or organization.

"Operationally, ideal family treatment begins when one can find a family leader with the courage to define self, who is invested in the welfare of the family as in self, who is neither angry nor dogmatic, whose energy goes to changing self rather than telling others what they should do, who can know and respect the multiple opinions of others, who can modify self in response to the strengths of the group, and who is not influenced by the irresponsible opinions of others. When one family member moves tower 'differentiation', the family symptoms disappear. A family leader is beyond the popular notion of power. A responsible family leader automatically generates mature leadership qualities in other family members who are to follow."[6]

It is the differentiated leader's ability not to get caught in the anxiety of the group that allows the leader to remain calm, neutral, reflective, and therefore, have a beneficial influence on the system. Like the ripples in a pond produced by one pebble, a differentiated leader's presence can send ripples and resonance during a conversation, meeting, or public event. The impact can even occur virtually.

Edwin Friedman describes such a leader in this way. "The basic concept of leadership through self-differentiation is this: If a leader will take primary responsibility for his or her own position as 'head' and work to define his or her own goals and self, while staying in touch with the rest of the organism, there is a more than reasonable chance that the body will follow. There may be initial resistance, but if the leader can stay in touch with the resisters, the body will usually go along."[7]

Orchestrating Conflict

In their book *Leadership on the Line,* leadership authorities Ron Heifetz and Marty Linksy consider leadership a risky business since effective leadership usually invites change, challenges the familiar, upsets routines, raises new questions, and disturbs current ways of thinking. Yet this is the nature of leadership, to make a difference in the lives of the people you lead and address difficult issues. Heifetz and Linksy believe that "the challenge of leadership when trying to generate adaptive change is to work with differences, passions, and conflicts in a way that diminishes their destructive potential and constructively harnesses their energy."[8] Heifetz and linksy use the term "orchestrating the conflict" for the role of effective leadership when facing challenge and conflict and outline strategies for harnessing the tension and energy to promote productive change.

Create a Holding Environment. Create a space that allows people to do the tough work. It includes boundaries around the size of the group(s), structures, procedures, rhythms, whatever allows people to address the issues productively.

Control the Temperature. Raise the tension level (temperature) enough to create attention, urgency, and the ability to act. However, the key is to keep the tension at a productive level. Too much pressure can either immobilize people (passive, inactive) or cause a group to lose control. Leadership takes steps to either calm things down (slow the pace, add more structure) or ramp it up (ask tough questions, give people more responsibility).

Pace the Work. Since people can only handle so much information and change, pace the work at a rate people can absorb and accept. This might include letting ideas seep out a little at a time. Delaying the most difficult issues and decisions for later allows confidence to build by handling the easier issues first.

Show Them the Future. To keep the momentum, remind people of the vision they are working toward and the values they are upholding. By imagining the future, it may seem more possible.

Give the Work Back. Giving the work back to the people indicates that they own the process and the responsibility for the work and the outcome. It reduces the pressure on the leader and the tendency to make the leader the target of anxiety for how things turn out.

Hold Steady. Resist the pressure of anxiety which makes everything seem urgent and heightens the need for a quick fix. Take time to reflect, evaluate, and make course corrections.[9] In the words of Adrienne Maree Brown, "Move at the speed of trust."[10]

A Case Study: Impasse at Lost River

"On our current trajectory, we have eighteen months before our reserves are depleted and we default on our mortgage," is not the statement any pastor hopes to say to their congregation at a quarterly business meeting. The unfortunate truth was that this was painful, but not surprising, news. The congregation had struggled with conflict and decline for more than a decade before I, Austin Almaguer, arrived as Senior Pastor. Unable and unwilling to make significant changes to its annual budget and spending practices, the congregation was depleting its reserves to meet budget each year. It would have been easy to point the finger at poor financial management as the reason for the congregation's current troubles. But as we know from Bowen Theory, this would be to mistake the presenting issue for the underlying emotional process that created the crisis. Conflict avoidance, quick fixes, and a lack of clarity in vision (congregational self-definition) created a culture of chronic anxiety that paralyzed action to address root causes.

Two years before I stood before the congregation with dire financial news, I started my first day of work as a first-call pastor at Vienna Baptist Church. The anxiety in the congregation, after two consecutive pastorates ended in painful departures, was palpable. The most common Biblical metaphor congregation members used to describe the congregation at the time was "the Israelites wandering in the desert." Afraid of losing any more members and experiencing any more pain, the congregation was motivated by a desire to please everyone. Choosing the direction of a congregation by unanimous consensus only benefits the most polarizing members who can hold progress hostage. While I was made aware of the financial instability of the congregation early in my tenure (although not the crisis we would ultimately face), I recognized the most important issue facing the congregation was self-definition. We needed to be clear on who we were called to be (identity), why we existed (vision), what we felt called to do (mission), and how we would we live out our purpose (strategic plan).

After a year of listening to the congregation through individual meetings and building relationships of trust, I organized a team of lay leaders to facilitate a strategic planning process for the congregation. The eighteen-month journey produced a new mission statement, "changing lives and transforming our community with the love of God," and shifted the congregation from an inward focus on the past and surviving toward an outward focus on the future and thriving.

We were concluding this process and preparing to plan a fun launch event when a series of shifts in the major donors of the congregation and economic factors dramatically changed our financial position. Suddenly, our multi-year timeline to patiently address our financial planning and management became a multi-month project to avoid foreclosure.

At the quarterly business meeting in June 2017, I framed the entire presentation around the changes necessary to live into this new sense of identity articulated in our mission statement. I focused on giving people language for controlling the temperature: we need not give in to panic nor avoid issues that must be confronted. I laid out a plan that would involve creating multiple teams of lay leaders to research various options in addressing our financial crisis. As a result, a broad base of the congregation was engaged in the work of addressing the problem instead of expecting the pastor to do the work for them (and ultimately laying the blame on that person when people didn't like the proposed plan).

For the next five months, teams worked at a steady pace examining everything from spending patterns to property sales. My role was to work with a team of three highly trusted and respected lay leaders to coordinate the work of teams and synthesize their findings. As our work progressed, it became clear that our mortgage was the single greatest drag on our annual budget ($127,000 per year). If we could eliminate our $785,000 mortgage debt, we would no longer have only eighteen months of financial viability. But we are a mid-size congregation without the ability to raise that much money that fast. What could we do? The answer came from one of our financial study teams that had been conducting research on the state of a retreat center our congregation owned in West Virginia.

There is a much longer and fascinating case study to be done on the Lost River Retreat Center (LRRC) for another time. Suffice it to say, while many long-time members had cherished memories of weekend retreats at LRRC from days long since passed which carried significant emotional weight, it was no longer a vibrant and active ministry of the congregation. The study team had initially begun a review of LRRC to understand the cost of needed repairs and improvements to test the viability of making it a revenue-generating property for the congregation, but it became clear that we could not afford the investment given our current financial reality. The study team also didn't feel it was a wise investment given our renewed focus on local community engagement as part of our mission statement to divert our attention across state lines for a ministry focused on our wants rather than local community needs. In fact, interest and use of the retreat center had declined over the years and enlisting volunteers to host events became more difficult.

While it was never their initial intent, the study team came to believe the best course of action was for the congregation to sell LRRC and use the revenue from the sale to retire our mortgage debt. The recommendation was wise but risky. During the study process, I had been advised by many long-time members not to even suggest selling the retreat center because it was a job killer. "Many years ago," I heard more than once, "a former pastor mentioned selling LRRC as an option and not long after he had to resign. Don't let that happen to you." Despite the risk, the study team and I knew this was our best option to address our current financial challenges so we could move forward with local ministry.

In November 2017, in the early morning hours
before our major congregational meeting where our
leadership team would publicly announce for the first time
the recommendation to sell the beloved Lost River Retreat
Center, I sent an email to the leadership team informing
them I would not be in attendance as my wife had gone
into labor with our first child. I assured the lay leaders that
I trusted them completely to lead this meeting on their
own and facilitate thoughtful conversation. While I stood
by my wife's side as we welcomed our daughter into the
world, the lay leaders served as midwives for the
congregation's own discernment in choosing what
sacrifices they would be willing to make to give life to our
new vision and mission. I would learn later that it was a
crucial conversation filled with honesty, vulnerability,
sorrow, and hope. At the end of the conversation, the
congregation was clear about moving forward with selling
Lost River to retire our debt and be freed to pursue our
shared mission.

As a leader, it was a moment when I had to trust
the people to discern the way forward for themselves. In
the days and weeks after returning from parental leave, I
spent time in the living rooms of congregation members
for whom I knew the decision to sell LRRC was personally
painful. In the home of one family who had invested
countless hours volunteering and attending retreats over
the years, I listened to them share their grief but also their

hope. "I'm so sad this has to happen," the adult daughter said, "but I want to thank you for this process. Every time selling Lost River has come up in the past, it's always been a quick fix someone has offered. But this process has been filled with prayer and listening. I may not like what we have to do, but I believe in our vision and I'm so excited for our commitment to help local families. If that's what this sale will help us do, then I'm in support." In that moment, she perfectly articulated a shift that others were experiencing. We were making decisions from a position of self-definition rather than reaction. The sale of the retreat center became a legacy gift for our future as a faith community. This was a necessary change so we could become the people we wanted to be.

We would later hold a special prayer service at Lost River to celebrate our memories on that sacred ground and all the people who invested so much of themselves in the ministry over the years. We were fortunate that the new owners were quick to honor the legacy of the property and we have since partnered with them to host a number of retreats for our community. On Sunday, November 4, 2018, I stood in the sanctuary on the spot where the year before I had defined the challenge before us, to celebrate our congregation being debt free for the first time in over thirty years. But we celebrated more than just a new financial position, we celebrated a new sense of self and a new commitment to make necessary changes to live out this identity more fully. This clarity and commitment continue to birth new ministries and remind us of the transformational power within orchestrating conflict well.

Conflict handled well brought opportunities to both congregation and church leaders at Vienna Baptist Church. Orchestrating conflict offered the congregation the best chance to clarify and develop its identity, mission, and vision as a faith community. The success of leaning into this challenging time increased the congregations' courage and confidence which may allow them to meet the next challenge with energy and resolve.

For church leaders, orchestrating conflict provided a training ground for self-development and leadership development, as they were invited to bring their whole selves to the effort. At the town hall in 2017, study team members stepped up to lead, define self, articulate values and beliefs, and recommend possible goals from their findings to an anxious gathering. It was a risky situation with the outcome uncertain.

Lawrence Matthews, former pastor of Vienna Baptist and founder of Leadership in Ministry, sums it up well. "The payoff of leadership through self-differentiation may not be what we think such a supposedly more insightful understanding of leadership ought to deliver – success of the endeavor and approval for the leader. This understanding of leadership focuses upon the leader and not upon the outcome of the leader's efforts. Viewed through the emotional process lens of family systems theory, 'leadership' is not about 'them' or 'success' but about self – self-regulation, self-definition, self-differentiation. The payoff is self."[11]

NOTES

[1]Murray Bowen, *Family Therapy in Clinical Practice* (Northvale, NJ: Jason Aronson, 1978), p. 485.

[2]Michael E. Kerr, *Bowen Theory's Secrets: Revealing the Hidden Life of Families* (New York: W.W. Norton & Co., 2019), pp. 32-33.

[3]Murray Bowen, *Family Therapy in Clinical Practice* (Northvale, NJ: Jason Aronson, 1978).

[4]Kathleen Smith, *Everything Isn't Terrible: Conquer Your Insecurities, Interrupt Your Anxiety, and Finally Calm Yourself Down* (New York: Hachette Books, 2019), p. 50.

[5]Peter L. Steinke, *Congregational Leadership in Anxious Times: Being Calm and Courageous No Matter What* (Herndon, VA: Alban Institute, 2006), p. 106.

[6]Michael E. Kerr & Murray Bowen, *Family Evaluation* (New York: W.W. Norton & Co, 1988), pp. 342–343.

[7]Edwin H. Friedman, *Generation to Generation: Family Process in Church and Synagogue* (New York: The Guilford Press, 1985), p. 229.

[8]Ronald A. Heifetz and Marty Linksy, *Leadership on the Line: Staying Alive through the Dangers of Leading* (Boston, MA: Harvard Business Review Press, 2002), p. 102.

[9]Ronald A. Heifetz and Marty Linsky, *Leadership on the Line: Staying Alive through the Dangers of Leading* (Boston, MA: Harvard Business Review Press, 2002).

[10]Adrienne Maree Brown, *Emergent Strategy* (Chico, CA: AK Press, 2017), p. 42.

[11]Lawrence E. Matthews, "Leadership Through a Bowen Systems Lens," in *Leadership in Ministry: Bowen Theory in the Congregational Context,* ed. Israel Galindo (Didache Press, 2017), p. 15.

15

Reframing Staff Leadership

Margaret Marcuson

T he last several years have made congregational staff relations even more complex and challenging than they were before. Pastors and staff are facing reduced numbers of volunteers and participants, while working even harder. Now more than ever, staff relations and staff leadership in congregations is not about changing others but about getting clear about your own principles, role, and goals; staying appropriately connected with those you lead; and keeping relatively calm throughout. Bowen Family Systems Theory offers a way to get beyond the personnel manual to the deep personal growth opportunity that staff relations provides.

This chapter will address three key questions:

1. How is staff leadership an opportunity for differentiation of self?
2. What makes for a well-functioning staff team?

3. How can Bowen theory help staff leaders navigate hiring, firing, and supervision?

The concepts from Bowen theory informing this chapter are differentiation of self, triangles, sibling position, identified patient, and overfunctioning/underfunctioning reciprocity

How can congregational staff leadership be an opportunity to work on differentiation of self?

It's tempting to view staff leadership as a way to change staff and get them to (take your pick): see the bigger picture, do their job, stay in their lane, or quit gossiping. Instead, the key element in effective leadership is to keep your focus on yourself and what Murray Bowen called differentiation of self. From that framework you focus on 1) your own clarity and 2) your connection with others, without trying to pressure or change others. Despite the challenges, staff relationships are an opportunity to grow in your ability to be a mature and well-functioning self. It's the biggest contribution you can make.

Bowen defined differentiation as, "…the degree to which one is able to balance (a) emotional and intellectual functioning (along with) (b) intimacy and autonomy in relationships." In addition, it is, "…the ability to distinguish thoughts from feelings, and to choose between being guided by one's intellect or one's emotions."[1] Differentiation, put simply, is being clear about your own thoughts, principles and values and being able to relate to others even when they differ. For example, one pastoral leader supervised a youth leader who had almost completely shut down during the early COVID-19 pandemic. The pastor said to him, "I know you can't do your job in the same way it was done. However, I believe it's important to stay connected with youth and their families now more than ever, and I'm asking you to develop new ways to reach out."

Working on differentiation includes developing awareness of the difference between thoughts and feelings, and being able to make choices about how to respond. It involves being principled but not rigid, connected but free from the need to be everyone's best friend. This balance is always a matter of degree, and rarely easy. We learn how to relate to others in the families we grow up in. I left home with patterns of relating that deeply affected how I related to staff as a pastor. I could share where I wanted to go as a leader. As an oldest daughter, that wasn't hard. What was hard was giving feedback to staff when things weren't working. I had to learn how to be more candid. I didn't have many examples in my family of how to do this.

Reflecting on your family of origin and how it affects your functioning and your leadership is a lifelong journey. Leaders who want to learn how to lead in differentiated ways can benefit from working with a coach. (The Leadership in Ministry workshops are one excellent resource for doing this work over time.)

Differentiation of self as a leader includes defining to staff the bigger picture as you see it and communicating where you are headed. Leaders have the opportunity to say first, "Here are my most important principles." Second, they can clarify, "Here's where I'm headed now, and here's what I want us to focus on."

Managing yourself in relation to the inevitable pushback goes with the territory of differentiated leadership. When it comes, you continue to be clear about the direction you are headed, without getting caught up in what "they" are or aren't doing. This seems counterintuitive, but continuing to bring your focus back to yourself and what you will and won't do will, over time, lead to better staff functioning.

Differentiation does not mean taking a stand and sticking with it at all costs in the name of "outlasting the resistance." It does mean staying in relationship and adjusting appropriately in response to feedback. Rev. Joe Clifford, senior pastor at Myers Park Presbyterian Church, put it this way, "Staff leadership affords opportunities to work on [differentiation] by challenging you to define self with those you manage and are working with to be clear in your vision and your expectations. And when there are problems, to have the capacity to engage those problems directly, honestly, non-anxiously, and to stay connected through the process, which can be really hard." Clifford adds, "I can have a tendency not to want to cause trouble, and that in itself will create anxiety in the system."[2]

I have found in my coaching practice as well as in my own ministry that clergy don't want to cause trouble. I've had to push myself to lean into my anxiety about "causing trouble" by having difficult conversations. As a young pastor, I worked with a church administrator who was nice and well-intentioned but chronically late. I knew nothing about Bowen theory, and like many pastors I had no training in staff supervision. I was also nice and well-intentioned but hated speaking up on difficult matters. I knew at a minimum that I had to speak with her about her tardiness. I had to force myself to say, "I need you to get to work on time." As simple as the sentence was and as basic the expectation, it was a differentiating opportunity for me. And she did change her behavior and started arriving on time.

Every staff configuration offers opportunities to work on differentiation.

What makes for a well-functioning staff team?

When you are clear about roles and goals, a better outcome is easier to achieve in any organization, as my consulting mentor, Rob Schachter, a long-time student of Bowen theory, repeated over and over. To the degree staff members know where you and the church are headed and what you expect of them, they are more likely to function well in their roles.

First, get clear yourself about expectations and then communicate them honestly with your staff. It goes with the job of pastor. Second, take the time to maintain connection, the relationship side of differentiation. It's worth the time to make sure you have at least a brief conversation with key staff members regularly--and with all staff, if you have a small staff. In addition, set limits with staff who want to take up a lot of your time--keep it in balance.

Staff Triangles

Understanding and navigating your position in staff triangles is essential for a well-functioning team. The concept of triangles is a basic Bowen theory idea. These are relationship or emotional triangles (not geometric triangles). Bowen suggested a two-person relationship is inherently unstable. One of the parties will pull in a third person to manage the anxiety in the relationship.[3] Typically, two members of the triangle are closer, and one is on the outside. Triangles are everywhere and are not in themselves problematic. They are a common way humans

handle relationships. Certain triangles go with the job—
they are functional. One example is the triangle between
the senior pastor, the staff, and the board. You become part
of the triangle when you take the job.

All pastors who have at least one staff member are
in triangles involving the staff. Israel Galindo says,
"Assume that whenever you are speaking with someone in
your congregation you are in a triangle… Nothing is ever
about 'just' you and the person."[4] This is also true about
everyone on your staff. Whenever you are speaking with
someone on your staff, you are in a triangle, with another
staff member, with a congregant, or a family member.
That's the reality of relationships on the job.

Triangles cause problems in team functioning
when anxiety rises and one or more people anxiously pull
in others, creating more (interlocking) triangles. For
example, the board makes a policy decision that the pastor
communicates to the staff. The functional triangle exists:
pastor-staff-board. One staff member disagrees with the
decision, because it affects his job responsibilities. He
complains to his wife—and further, to the lay leadership
team he works with whose members then pull in others
spreading the complaint around the church. One triangle
(board-pastor-staff) has become multiple interlocking
anxiety-driven triangles.

Joe Clifford suggests, "The leader is the outside
party in triangles on multi-staff teams…. I think there can

become unhealthy triangles where you get closer to some staff than others, and so you find yourself talking with each other about a third party, and that can generate anxiety in the system if there's not direct communication." In the case above, the pastor might vent to the associate, while avoiding a conversation with the triangling staff member, thus increasing the interlocking triangles further. This can even happen on a staff of three, where the pastor complains about the custodian to the administrator.

As a pastor I found when I was overwhelmed or confused, I could get more clarity and calm by sitting down with a piece of paper and diagraming the triangles. Me-secretary-custodian. Oh, I'm taking responsibility for their relationship. Me-staff-executive board (about the budget and salaries). Oh, I'm taking responsibility for whether they get a raise or not. Then I'd add the interlocking triangles with the families of the staff. The exercise of diagramming helped me be clear about where my responsibility was—and, just as important, where it wasn't.

Sibling Position

Take the time to learn the sibling position of all the members of your staff. This is another Bowen theory concept that can help make for a well functioning team. This concept suggests birth order and sibling position can have a significant influence on how people function. Knowing the birth order of team members—and your own—can be useful in maximizing the strengths and navigating the pitfalls of staff relations. As a conforming oldest daughter, I can be bossy and controlling, yet I hate to make waves—it's a double bind. I've had to learn to manage both those tendencies.

One younger born pastor noticed he has to work hard to do the work of defining self and setting a direction for the team. A staff member in that church, an oldest-born music director, could discipline herself to step back and allow the pastoral team to make decisions about worship she disagrees with. The pastor is aware of this and makes sure he is able to stand up to her in these decisions without getting too reactive about her immediate response. He knows she is mature enough to accept it without making a big fuss.

Another pastor was an oldest daughter whose parents were both youngest children. She was so used to no one in the family taking responsibility but herself that she didn't even notice the associate pastor was falling short in his responsibilities. Lay leaders pointed it out, and she was then able to step up and take needed action.

The most important framework is to be aware of your own sibling position and manage your go-to anxious responses. However, keeping the position of others on your radar can help you be less reactive to their automatic responses.[5]

Hiring and Supervision

How do leaders navigate hiring, firing, and supervision? Good hiring, supervision, and, yes, firing practices are essential to a well-functioning staff team.

No hiring process is foolproof. However, you can view the process itself as an opportunity for differentiation of self: define yourself to the candidate and to anyone else (for example, the personnel committee) involved in the process. You can also encourage candidates to do the same in return by asking thoughtful questions.

Look for personal maturity as much as the skills for the job. Colleen Barrett, former CEO of Southwest Airlines, said, "We literally say that we hire for attitude and we train for skill." Pilots had to have the appropriate skills, but if they didn't have the right attitude, they didn't get hired.[6]

If the applicant pool isn't big enough, go with the best attitude and the most maturity. You don't want a tone-deaf choir director, but a less-skilled director who is open to your input on worship will be much better for the congregation than one with a Juilliard degree who isn't. Whatever the position, church staff members need to be able to work with others.

Supervision is itself an opportunity to work on differentiation. Like having a teenager in the house, supervising a challenging employee can teach you a lot about yourself. Susan Beaumont, co-author of *When Moses Met Aaron: Staffing and Supervision in Large Congregations*, suggests, "Supervision, like any other task of leadership, relies on the art of the use of self... Supervision is an invitation into greater self awareness." With challenging employees, she suggests you ask yourself, "Why is this making me crazy?" Or, "Why do I have this one staff member I just find it impossible to get along with? This person just presses every button I have."[7]

Bowen theory suggests it can be useful to consider how this "difficult" employee resembles someone in your family of origin (immediate or extended) and inquire of yourself what's setting you off. It might have less to do with that person in the office than you think. In addition, you can notice the people you are most in tune with and enjoy working with the most. Can you get enough distance to effectively supervise them? That presents another challenge.

What about hiring and supervising church members? Some suggest never hiring church members. But let's be honest—churches hire members all the time. Clarifying the difference between "staff member" and "church member" is critical when someone has both roles. When they are at work, they are primarily a staff member.

They are supervised as a staff member not a church member. This can be a challenge for pastors. It's important to develop some principles for yourself. Susan Beaumont says pastors need to understand "a supervisory relationship is actually different when the person is also a member. Their primary allegiance needs to be to their employment relationship.... The biggest problem I see is [pastors] getting that mixed up in their heads, because they can't discipline, they can't fire people."[8]

Overfunctioning and underfunctioning

The work of supervision gives an opportunity to manage the tendency to overfunction. Overfunctioning is a reciprocal behavior between those who take too much responsibility and those who don't take enough responsibility. Working hard on your own job and your own goals is not overfunctioning. It takes two (or more) to engage in overfunction/underfunction reciprocity. Working long hours at least for a time does not necessarily mean overfunctioning. Working a lot harder than the rest of the staff, never taking a day off or not taking all of your vacation may mean you are overfunctioning.

In staff relations, substantial amounts of time and attention can be given to an underfunctioning employee to get them to improve their performance. In other instances, the pastor and other staff members work around the problem employee, taking on more work for themselves in the process. What to do instead? Continue to define yourself and your expectations in a neutral way, and then observe the response over time. Can people change their behavior in response to feedback? With other employees, supervision may involve coaching them to do less when they are picking up the slack for others.

Even with staff who are not members, clergy can overfunction pastorally. If a staff member has personal challenges, you can be open to offering support and a certain degree of flexibility through a difficult time. But remember, your primary role with them is as an employer. You don't have hours to spend with them, except in an emergency. You can't afford for them to spend hours of work time talking about their problems or to take months off work. They were hired to do a job, which they need to do. Many clergy find it hard to make demands of staff who are underfunctioning, whether or not they are church members.

Underfunctioning or recalcitrant employees can function on a church staff like the notion of the "identified patient." In a family, when a problem in an individual comes up, it is not simply an individual symptom, but a symptom for the family. In a congregation, a problem person, including a problem staff member, is expressing something for the larger body. There's an opening for this kind of behavior.[9]

When you view an underfunctioning employee as
an "identified patient," you still have to address the
employee directly—avoiding anxious triangles. However,
there are wider systemic issues at work. For example, one
church with substantial resources couldn't seem to hire a
competent business manager--for several decades. It
turned out the same controlling lay leaders were on the
finance committee for all of that time, and they wouldn't
allow the business manager the authority even to sign the
checks. It wasn't until the church hired a favorite son of the
church that they were able to ensure the position had the
authority it needed for increased success. If you have one
position that always seems to be problematic, get curious
about the history. How have people in the position
functioned over the years—even decades?

Letting people go

At times you will have to let people go. For pastors
who learned from their families to be nice, to soothe the
feelings of others, and to overfunction, this can be difficult.
However, heads of staff have the responsibility to the
larger organization. The job requires leaning into the
uncomfortable feelings that go with letting someone go. In
many congregations, depending on polity, you may want
to bring in key lay leaders as part of the decision-making
process. This differs from anxiously triangling by

complaining. Instead, it's making strategic use of triangles to share responsibility for important decisions. When you fire someone, you may find it's a relief when it's done. As one pastor noted, "I didn't realize how much energy this person was taking until he was gone."

What if you inherit a staff member who is unfireable, at least for now? Pastors can arrive to find a key staff member, often a long-tenured secretary or music director, has so much influence in the congregation that a new pastor can't make a move. What to do? Work on your relationship with them, without appeasing them. Work on your internal reactivity to them. Keep defining yourself in a calm way. And work to establish relationships with other key players in the congregation. If you stay calm, you'll likely outlast them.

The ongoing work of differentiation in staff relations is to keep defining self, staying in relationship and managing your own anxious reactivity. There's always something to keep you on your toes.

Staff leadership provides an opportunity to work on differentiation of self. Taking the time to understand yourself in relation to your staff—what are your own family of origin patterns and triggers, and looking for opportunities to define yourself and stay connected, will go a long way toward making for effective staff functioning. When you are clear about your own purpose and goals, stay in open contact with key staff members, and manage your own emotional life so you can remain relatively calm, or at least calm yourself down as needed, staff relations will go better. As St. Paul said, "If it is possible, so far as it depends on you, live peaceably with all" (Romans 12:18, NRSV). Not everyone will like you or your ideas, but you can manage your side of all of these relationships. Attending to hiring, supervision, and dismissing, and being clear about what's expected and what are the implications will lead to a calmer and more productive staff environment.

NOTES

[1]Murray Bowen, *Family Therapy in Clinical Practice,* (Aronson, 1978).

[2]Personal interview, November 30, 2022.

[3]Bowen, *Family Therapy in Clinical Practice,* p. 306-307.

[4]Israel Galindo, *Perspectives on Congregational Leadership* (Educational Consultants, 2013), p. 22.

[5]For more on this, see Margaret Marcuson, "On Sibling Position," in *Leadership in Ministry: Bowen Theory in the Congregational Context* (Didache Press, 2017), pp. 18ff.

[6]https://knowledge.wharton.upenn.edu/article/southwest-airlines-colleen-barrett-flies-high-on-fuel-hedging-and-servant-leadership/

[7]Personal Interview, January 17, 2023.

[8]See Gil Rendle and Susan Beaumont, *When Moses Met Aaron* (Alban, 2007), chapter 2 for more on employment relationships with members.

[9]Edwin Friedman, *Generation to Generation* (Guilford Press, 1985), pp. 19-20.

Bibliography

Belenky, Mary Field, et al. *Women's Ways of Knowing: The Development of Self, Voice, and Mind.* New York: Basic Books, Inc., 1986.

Bendroth, Norman. *Interim Ministry in Action.* Lanham MD. Rowman & Littlefield, 2018.

Bendroth, Norman. *Rethinking Interim Ministry,* posted at https://alban.org/archive/rethinking-transitional-ministry/.

Bowen, Murray. *Family Therapy in Clinical Practice.* Northvale, NJ: Jason Aronson, Inc., 1993.

_____. *The Origins of Family Psychotherapy: The NIMH Family Study Project.* Edited by J. Butler. New York: Jason Aronson, 2013.

Boyce, Andy and Dreelin, Andrew. "Ecologists Dig Prairie Dogs, and You Should Too." *Smithsonian's National Zoo & Conservation Biology Institute.* Jul 02, 2020. https://nationalzoo.si.edu/ conservation-ecology-center/news/ecologists-dig-prairie-dogs-and-you-should-too. MacDonald, D. "Helpers' in Fox Society." Nature 282, (1979): 69–71. See also https://doi.org/10.1038/282069a0. "Naked Mole-rat: Heterocephalus glaber." Sand Diego Zoo. 2003. https://animals.sandiegozoo.org/animals/naked-mole-rat.

Brown, Adrienne Maree. *Emergent Strategy.* Chico, CA: AK Press, 2017.

Brown, Jenny. *Growing Yourself Up: How to bring your best self to all of life's relationships.* Australia: Exisle Publishing Pty, Ltd., 2017.

Brown, Lyn Mikel and Carol Gilligan, *Meeting at the Crossroads: Women's Psychology and Girl's Development.* Cambridge, MA: Harvard University Press, 1992.

Buzsáki, György. "How the Brain 'Constructs' the Outside World," Scientific American (June 1, 2022).

Chittister, Joan. *The Rule of Benedict.* New York: Crossroad, 1992.

Clebsch, William A. and Charles R. Jaekle, *Pastoral Care in Historical Perspective.* Englewood Cliffs, NY, Prentice-Hall, 1964.

Craddock, Fred "Pastoral Preaching," in *Dictionary of Pastoral Care and Counseling,* ed. Rodney J. Hunter. Nashville, Abingdon Press, 1990.

Dolan, Jay P. "Patterns of Leadership in the Congregation," in James P. Wind, and James W. Lewis, eds., *American Congregations.* Vol. 2: New Perspectives in the Study of Congregations. Chicago: The University of Chicago Press, 1994.

Friedman, Edwin H. *A Failure of Nerve: Leadership in the Age of the Quick Fix.* Margaret M. Treadwell, and Edward W. Beal, eds., New York: Seabury Books, 2007.

_____. *Family Process and Process Theology.* Alban Institute, 1991. Videocassette.

_____. *Generation to Generation: Family Process in Church and Synagogue.* New York, Guilford Press, 1985.

Gaarden, Marianne. *The Third Room of Preaching: The Sermon, The Listener, and the Creation of Meaning.* Westminster John Knox Press, 2017.

Galindo, Israel, Elaine Boomer, and Don Reagan. *A Family Genogram Workbook.* Educational Consultants, 2017.

Galindo, Israel. *101 System Theory Quotes.* Didache Press, 2016.

_____. *Perspectives on Congregational Leadership.* Richmond VA. Educational Consultants, 2013.

_____. *The Hidden Lives of Congregations: Understanding Congregational Dynamics.* Herndon, VA: Alban Institute, 2004.

Gilbert, Roberta M. *Extraordinary Relationships: A New Way of Thinking About Human Interactions.* New York: John Wiley & Sons, Inc., 1992.

_____. *Connecting with Our Children.* New York: John Wiley & Sons Inc. 2008.

Goleman, Daniel, Richard Boyatzis, and Annie McKee, *Primal Leadership: Realizing the Power of Emotional Intelligence.* Boston: Harvard Business School Press, 2002.

Gurman, Alan S. and David Kniskern, eds. *Handbook of Family Therapy,* Vol. 2. New York: runner/Mazel, 1991.

Heifetz, Ronald A. and Marty Linksy, *Leadership on the Line: Staying Alive through the Dangers of Leading.* Boston, MA: Harvard Business Review Press, 2002.

_____. *Leadership Without Easy Answers.* Cambridge, MA: Belknap Press of Harvard University Press, 1994.

Hiltner, Seward. *Preface to Pastoral Theology.* Nashville, Abingdon Press, 1958.

Hollander, E. P. "Conformity, Status and Idiosyncrasy Credit." *Psychological Review* 65 (1958).

Kerr, Michael and Murray Bowen. *Family Evaluation: An Approach Based on Bowen Theory.* W. W. Norton & Company, 1988.

_____. *Bowen Theory's Secrets: Revealing the Hidden Life of Families.* New York: W.W. Norton & Company, 2019.

_____. *One Family's Story: A Primer on Bowen Theory.* Georgetown Family Center, 2017.

Luff, Susan. "Overfunctioning Leadership Gone Awry." Lecture presented at the Postgraduate Clergy Seminar in Family Emotional Process, Bethesda, Maryland, October 26, 1995.

Machado, Antonio. *Border of a Dream.* Trans. by Willis Barnstone. Copper Canyon Press, 2004

Marcuson, Margaret. "On Sibling Position," in *Leadership in Ministry: Bowen Theory in the Congregational Context.* Didache Press, 2017.

Matthews, Lawrence E. "Leadership Through a Bowen Systems Lens," in *Leadership in Ministry: Bowen Theory in the Congregational Context.* Ed. Israel Galindo. Didache Press, 2017.

May, Gerald "Don't Be a Pest," *Shalem News*, Vol. 21, No. 2 Summer 1997.

Mead, Loren. *A Change of Pastors.* Herndon, VA Alban, 2005.

Mills, L.O. "Pastoral Care (History, Traditions, and Definitions)," in *Dictionary of Pastoral Care and Counseling,* ed. Rodney J. Hunter, (Nashville, Abingdon Press, 1990.

Morton, Nelle. *The Journey Is Home.* Boston: Beacon Press, 1985.

Nietzsche, Friedrich. *Thus Spoke Zarathustra.* Penguin Classics 1961.

Noone, Robert. *Family and Self: Bowen Theory and the Shaping of Adaptive Capacity.* New York: Lexington Books, 2021.

O'Connor, Mary-Frances. *The Grieving Brain.* New York: Harper One, 2022.

Overstreet, H.A. *The Mature Mind.* New York: W.W. Norton & Company, Inc., 1949.

Palmer, Parker. A *Hidden Wholeness; The Journey Toward an Undivided Life.* San Francisco: Jossy-Bass, 2004.

Papero, Daniel V., *Bowen Family Systems Theory.* Massachusetts: Allyn and Bacon, 1990.

Rendle, Gil and Alice Mann. *Holy Conversations: Strategic Planning as a Spiritual Practice for Congregations.* Alban Institute, 2003.

_____ and Susan Beaumont. *When Moses Met Aaron.* Herndon VA Alban, 2007.

Richardson, Ronald. *Becoming a Healthier Pastor.* Fortress Press, 2004.

_____. *Mothers and Sons: Changing the Script.* Independently Published, 2022.

Rowling, J.K. *The Casual Vacancy.* New York: Little Brown and Company, 2012.

Siegel, Daniel. *Parenting from the Inside Out.* New York: Penquin Putnam Inc., 2003.

Smith, Kathleen. *Everything Isn't Terrible: Conquer Your Insecurities, Interrupt Your Anxiety, and Finally Calm Yourself Down.* New York: Hachette Books, 2019.

Smith, Walter. "Emotional Cutoff and Family Stability: Child Abuse in Family Emotional Process" in *Emotional Cutoff: Bowen Family Systems Theory Perspectives,* edited by Peter Titelman. New York: The Haworth Clinical Practice Press, 2003.

Steinke, Peter L. *Congregational Leadership in Anxious Times: Being Calm and Courageous No Matter What.* Herndon, VA: Alban Institute, 2006.

Titelman, Peter. *Emotional Cutoff: Bowen Family Systems Theory Perspectives*. Routledge, 2003.

Tracy, Patricia. Jonathan Edwards, *Pastor: Religion and society in eighteenth-century Northampton*. Wipf and Stock Publishers, 2006.

Made in the USA
Columbia, SC
15 July 2023

20040967R00143